THE WORLD ALMANAC ALMANAC
PLACES TO GO
BEFORE YOU CAN'T

JOHN ROSENTHAL

WORLD ALMANAC BOOKS

T0035095

Copyright © 2023 by Skyhorse Publishing, Inc.

All rights reserved. No part of this book may be reproduced in any manner without the express written consent of the publisher, except in the case of brief excerpts in critical reviews or articles. All inquiries should be addressed to World Almanac, 307 West 36th Street, 11th Floor, New York, NY 10018.

World Almanac books may be purchased in bulk at special discounts for sales promotion, corporate gifts, fund-raising, or educational purposes. Special editions can also be created to specifications. For details, contact the Special Sales Department, 307 West 36th Street, 11th Floor, New York, NY 10018 or info@skyhorsepublishing.com.

Published by World Almanac, an imprint of Skyhorse Publishing, Inc., 307 West 36th Street, 11th Floor, New York, NY 10018.

The World Almanac is a trademark of Skyhorse Publishing, Inc. All rights reserved.

www.skyhorsepublishing.com

10 9 8 7 6 5 4 3 2 1

Text by John Rosenthal
Photos by Getty Images and Shutterstock, except page 254, The Muraka, Conrad Maldives Rangali Island
Interior design by Chris Schultz
Cover design by David Ter-Avanesyan
Cover images by Getty Images and Shutterstock

Library of Congress Cataloging-in-Publication Data is available on file.

Print ISBN: 978-1-5107-7382-0
Ebook ISBN: 978-1-5107-7383-7

Printed in China

Contents

Introduction

What an incredible time it is to be a traveler. Never in the history of humankind has it been possible to visit so many corners of the earth. From the far northern reaches of Canada to the most remote islands in Micronesia, there's not a spot on the planet that can't be reached by a determined visitor.

Stop for a moment to consider that fact in its historic context. When the ancient Greeks first enumerated their seven wonders of the ancient world in the first century BCE, the world as they knew it consisted only of the Mediterranean and the Middle East, and five of the seven landmarks celebrated Hellenic achievements in construction.

Two centuries later, the world is so much wider and so much more wonderful. But even though six of the seven ancient wonders were destroyed by fire, war, or earthquakes by 1303 CE, the Greeks' list continues to capture western imaginations. In the seven centuries since a massive tremor laid the Lighthouse of Alexandria to ruins, some world traveler may have updated the list to include the Great Wall of China, the Taj Mahal, or Machu Picchu, to name just a few. But if so, that roster hasn't survived. It's only in the past 30 years that organizations ranging from the American Society of Civil Engineers to *USA Today* to *Astronomy* magazine have started to rethink what constitutes a wonder—and also what constitutes the world, now that humans have circumnavigated the globe, plumbed the depths of the oceans, and voyaged to the farthest reaches of space. Meanwhile, a Swiss corporation calling itself the New7WondersFoundation set up a website in 2001 encouraging voters to choose not only a septet of the world's most monumental monuments, but also the seven most awe-inspiring natural wonders and the seven most spectacular cities.

But why stop at seven? That averages out to just one wonder per continent. Why not 17, 70, 700, or 7,000? International travel is cheaper, faster, and more accessible than ever, and people have more disposable income and leisure time than they did at any time in history. Moreover, as our life spans increase, so too should our bucket lists. In 1940, the average 65-year-old man could expect to live another 12 years, while the typical woman could anticipate 13 golden years; by 2022, those numbers had increased to 19 and 21. That's another seven-plus years to see the world.

The list of destinations in this book is by no means comprehensive. Notably absent are indisputable wonders like the Colosseum or Chichén Itzá. Instead, the focus is on places that are at risk of changing irrevocably, or even disappearing altogether. Sadly, the most imminent threat to so many of the selections is climate change. Rising seas, higher temperatures, rampant wildfires, and floods have already taken aim at some of the world's most beloved places, as well as the animals that call them home.

But other factors are at work too. Pompeii and the Taj Mahal, for example, are suffering from neglect. Logging, mining, and oil and gas exploration activities threaten natural treasures from Alaska to Zambia. Armed conflict in central Africa puts endangered mountain gorillas in the crosshairs. Burrowing moles could topple Stonehenge (seriously!). Skyscrapers might soon dwarf the historic architecture in the center of Vienna. Poachers, not pollution, are the greatest threats to Indonesia's endangered Komodo dragons. Route 66 is being erased faster than the Berlin Wall.

Not all impending changes are for the worse, however. After a devastating fire in 2019, Paris's Notre-Dame cathedral is rising from the ashes. In Barcelona, Antoni Gaudí's Sagrada Família nears completion, more than 140 years after its cornerstone was first laid. Vietnam, formerly one of the world's poorest countries, is urbanizing at an unprecedented rate. Lava reshapes the contours of Hawaii's Volcanoes National Park every day. And if you've got a quarter of a million bucks, it's now possible to dive down to the bottom of the Atlantic where you can see the wreck of the RMS *Titanic*.

So what are you waiting for? Get out there and see the world—before you can't.

—John Rosenthal

NORTH AMERICA

Big Sur

Drive one of the world's prettiest coastlines.

There's something magical about places where the mountains meet the sea. On islands like Oahu, Majorca, Moorea, and St. Lucia or knife-edges-of-the-continent like Acadia National Park, Italy's Amalfi Coast, and Australia's Great Ocean Road, the abrupt transition from land to water creates dramatic, rugged terrain.

Perhaps the most breathtaking such intersection is Big Sur, on California's central coast. Pacific Coast Highway (PCH) is the only road in and out of this gorgeous landscape, but the drive is so replete with outstanding vistas that you wouldn't want to take any other route.

Unless you're in a hurry, that is. This is definitely a scenic route, following the contours of the coast, twisting and turning sharply to reveal unexpected views in all directions. The best views of Big Sur's majesty, of course, are the ones without a windshield. Stop at Andrew Molera State Park

Plan Your Trip

Location: Central California coast, between Monterey and Cambria

Getting There: The closest major airports are San Jose International, about two hours north of Big Sur, or San Francisco International, another hour farther north.

When to Go: In general, the dry season between April and October sees the most visitors and the most expensive hotel rates. But the weather on the Central Coast is fickle. Like San Francisco, Big Sur can be shrouded by fog even on the hottest days of summer, or brilliantly sunny in the depths of the rainy season between November-March. The fog often—but not always—lifts by midday.

to hike through groves of towering redwoods, surf the clear—but chilly—ocean break, or learn

about the Ventana Wilderness Society's conservation efforts to return endangered California condors to the wild.

Julia Pfeiffer Burns State Park is home to two popular hikes, neither of which takes more than an hour. The Partington Cove trail goes over a bridge and through a tunnel in the cliff to reach a secluded grotto. The Overlook Trail leads to clifftop views of McWay Falls, where the water cascades onto a small beach.

Accommodations anywhere along this stretch mostly range from expensive to the down payment on a house. The 169 campsites at Pfeiffer Big Sur State Park cost $35 per night ($50 for riverfront locations) but usually fill up six months in advance.

About an hour south of Big Sur awaits a man-made attraction equal to the magnificence of the natural surroundings: Hearst Castle. Built by newspaper magnate William Randolph Hearst between 1919 and 1947, the ultra-opulent estate is now a museum and state park. Paintings, sculptures, tapestries, and Greek and Roman statues line the castle's gilded rooms and its two over-the-top swimming pools, where A-listers like Charlie Chaplin, Mary Pickford, Charles Lindbergh, Winston Churchill, and George Bernard Shaw spent the weekend as Hearst's guests.

In the past decade, heavy rains after forest fires have twice caused mudslides that wiped out portions of PCH near Big Sur. The first collapse, in 2017, took 14 months and $54 million to rebuild; in 2021, another slide closed the road for three months and cost $11 million to repair. At some point, this stretch of highway may become too expensive to maintain.

Napa Valley

Taste the wines of the Cabernet capital of the world, before it's too hot to grow grapes.

Long derided by oenophiles as inferior to the grand vineyards of Europe, California wines finally surpassed their French counterparts in 1976, when a panel of judges at the Paris Wine Tasting gave top honors to both a Chardonnay and a Cabernet Sauvignon from Napa Valley. The French media virtually ignored this sea-change, but the news set off shock waves in the U.S., burnishing the reputation of California's wine industry and turning sleepy Napa Valley into a premier travel destination.

Located less than 90 minutes northeast of San Francisco, Napa (the name of the valley as well as a town in the region) enjoys a Mediterranean climate ideal for wine growing. Fog rolling in from the Pacific Ocean keeps vineyards cool in the morning,

Plan Your Trip

Location: Northern California

Getting There: The closest airport is San Francisco International, about 90 minutes south and west of Napa.

When to Go: There's no bad time to visit Napa in terms of weather. It almost never rains between May and November and rarely gets uncomfortably hot. Harvest season (August-October) is one of the more popular times to visit, with hotel rates elevated accordingly.

while afternoons are sunny and warm, but not too hot. Once the sun goes down, the lack of humidity makes for cool, sometimes chilly, evenings. These conditions help grapes ripen slowly, developing complex aromas while preserving just the right amount of sugar and acidity.

More than 500 wineries line the bucolic roads and hillsides of this 192-square-mile (238-sq.-km) area, most specializing in the Cabernets and Chardonnays for which Napa first won international notice. But microclimates throughout the region have also created excellent conditions for growing Merlot, Pinot Noir, and Sauvignon Blanc, among others. Serious wine enthusiasts might spend an entire Napa Valley vacation doing nothing more than tasting wine and pairing it with exceptional food, as at Thomas Keller's The French Laundry in Yountville, which has been awarded three Michelin stars since 2006. But Napa's rolling hills between two mountain ranges are also a beautiful backdrop for hot air ballooning, kayaking the Napa River, bicycling the Silverado Trail, or soaking in natural hot springs.

As in some of France's wine-growing regions, climate change threatens to upset the delicate balance that makes Napa so ideal for producing wine. Wildfires in 2017 and 2020 burned thousands of acres and turned some wine grapes into expensive raisins. Even vineyards that were spared the heat and flames saw their grapes take on an ash flavor known as smoke taint. More ruined crops are in store if temperatures continue to rise at their current pace. By 2050, climatologists predict the temperature in Napa will exceed 100°F (38°C) more than 15 times a year, far too hot for Cabernet Sauvignon grapes. Some wineries may be able to mitigate the damage by switching to hardier grapes, but that won't completely offset the losses.

Yosemite

Get to know California's favorite park, up close and personal.

Even if you've never been to Yosemite, you probably think you know it. Maybe somebody bought you a calendar of Ansel Adams's iconic photos. Maybe you saw Alex Honnold scale El Capitan in the 2018 film *Free Solo*. Maybe you read about the time Teddy Roosevelt asked John Muir to personally guide him on a camping trip through the park—a visit that led to expanded federal protection of the Yosemite Valley and the creation of five more national parks and 150 national forests. Maybe you've seen postcards of sequoias so massive you could drive a car through a tunnel in one of their trunks.

But when you set foot in the park, you realize you hardly know it at all. As stunning as the Ansel Adams photos are, they can't capture in black and white the impossibly cerulean sky that brightens even amateur selfies. Unless you're a serious climber, you can only stand at the base of El Capitan and marvel at Honnold's ascent. And those colossal trees? They're in another section of the park, an hour's drive (albeit a pretty one) south of the locus of activity in Yosemite Valley (and you can't actually drive through any of them).

You also may not be prepared for the number of people that flood Yosemite's premier attractions from May through September. A pilot program starting in 2022 attempted seasonal crowd control by requiring visitors to secure a reservation to drive into the park between 6 AM and 4 PM. But to get that picture-perfect shot of Half Dome, Cathedral Rocks, or Yosemite Falls, you may still have to wait

Plan Your Trip

Location: Central California

Getting There: The closest major airport is in Fresno, about 2½ hours away by car. San Francisco International Airport is about a 3½-hour drive.

When to Go: More than three-quarters of all Yosemite visitors arrive between May and October; July and August are the busiest months. The roads to Glacier Point and Tuolumne Meadows close completely in winter. Yosemite's waterfalls peak in April and May but usually dry up by midsummer.

for a dozen or more other Adams wannabes to snap their photos. And you'll want to secure your lodgings far in advance, be they in a campground, cabin, motel, or the majestic, historic (and pricy) Ahwahnee Hotel.

None of this should deter you from getting to know Yosemite in person. Yosemite Valley gets most of the park's traffic, but it's only a tiny portion of the acreage. The farther you get from the valley, the more intimate your Yosemite experience will be. The park features more than 750 miles (1,208 km) of hiking trails, many of which ascend to breathtaking vistas you can't see from below. Seeing the park on a bicycle often allows you to whiz by cars stuck in traffic.

Unfortunately, those cars aren't just a traffic headache; they're a major source of air pollution that can turn those strikingly blue skies brown or gray. The worst smog usually comes from outside the park, carried by westerly winds from California's Central Valley. This ground-level ozone pollution is distinct from smoke from forest fires, also a now-constant threat. Fire season traditionally lasted from July to November but is nearly year-round these days because of climate change and drought.

Las Vegas

Enjoy Sin City before it truly becomes hellish.

Las Vegas is fabulous. There's even a sign at the entrance to the Strip swearing to it. And unlike so many things about Sin City, the promise of a fabulous vacation isn't just hype. Beyond the flashing neon, the spinning roulette wheels, and the pulsing beat at the legendary pool parties lie some attractions that truly make Las Vegas fabulous.

Ironically, gambling isn't even one of them. As of 2022, casinos were legal in more than 40 U.S. states, and in 24 of them, you don't even have to go to tribal land. If you want to play craps or blackjack you probably don't have to fly all the way to the middle of the desert. You do, however, need a special trip to see Adele in concert one night and Usher the next. Once a destination for fading stars trading on well-worn hits, today's Vegas is where A-list talent

takes up residency for sold-out months at a time. (And of course Wayne Newton, as ever.)

All-you-can-eat buffets are practically synonymous with Las Vegas, and there are still

Plan Your Trip

Location: Southern Nevada

Getting There: Harry Reid International Airport receives direct flights from all over the U.S.

When to Go: There's no wrong time to go if you plan to stay indoors. Temperatures get uncomfortably hot in summer (May-September), but hotel prices usually fall as the mercury rises.

plenty of them. But in recent years, steam tables have been supplemented by some of the best restaurants in the country. Just about every celebrity chef you can think of—from Emeril to Giada to Nobu—has a Vegas outpost. Their presence has created a dining scene that now rivals cities like New York, Los Angeles, and New Orleans, with options for every budget.

Visitors may also be surprised by how much of Las Vegas is free, and not just the drinks. It costs absolutely nothing to watch the dancing waters in the Bellagio fountain, tour the Wildlife Habitat at the Flamingo, experience the erupting volcano at the Mirage, wander the Forum Shops at Caesars Palace, or marvel at the kitschy architecture of Paris or the Luxor. Simply walking up and down the Strip (a.k.a. Las Vegas Blvd.) is one of the best travel values in the world.

But as the planet heats up, Vegas visitors might find themselves ever-more confined to swimming pools and air-conditioned spaces (ironically, contributing even more greenhouse gases to the problem). In 2022, Climate Central ranked Las Vegas as the second-fastest-warming city in the U.S., with summer temperatures rising 5.8°F (3.3°C) since 1970. The only city that heated up faster over that time period? Reno, where temperatures skyrocketed 10.9°F (6.1°C).

Grand Canyon

Just one look is all it takes to be spellbound.

There are all kinds of reasons *not* to visit Grand Canyon.

It's hot. From June to August, the mercury at the top of the canyon routinely crests 100°F (38°C), and it's often 20 degrees (11°C) hotter on the canyon floor.

It's cold. It gets below freezing most nights from November to April on the South Rim. It gets warmer as you descend into the canyon, but snow that melts and refreezes into ice can make footing treacherous.

It's crowded. Approximately 6 million people visit Grand Canyon each year. The wait to get into the park can be up to two hours, and parking can be scarce after 9 AM. Campsites and hotel rooms, especially those within the park, fill up months in advance.

There's nothing to do. There are only a few hiking trails at the South Rim, usually ranging from steep to very steep. Most of them save the hardest part of the journey for last, when you walk back up the canyon. And you have to keep an eye out to avoid stepping in mule poop.

So why is Grand Canyon on everyone's bucket list? Because even a brief visit to this ginormous hole in the ground just might change your world view. Here lies 6 million years of history, unearthed millimeter by millimeter by the Colorado River,

Plan Your Trip

Location: Northern Arizona

Getting There: Phoenix's Sky Harbor International Airport is a 3.5-hour drive from the South Rim. The closest airport to the North Rim is Harry Reid International in Las Vegas (about five hours by car).

When to Go: The shoulder seasons (April-May and Sept.-Oct.) are the best time to visit. The weather is not too hot and not too cold, and there are far fewer crowds than in the peak summer season (June-August).

until the entire state of Rhode Island could fit inside this mile- (1.6-km-) deep chasm. Doing nothing more than gaping at what nature hath wrought is a humbling experience. No wonder it's been named one of the seven natural wonders of the world.

So if it's hot, take a rafting trip down the river, stay in the air-conditioned car and follow the 23-mile (37-km) Desert View Drive, or feel the breeze as you bicycle the 13-mile (22-km) Greenway, which connects the South Rim's most popular destinations. If it's cold, warm up with a brisk walk along Canyon Rim Trail, which traces the south rim for 13 miles (22 km) and is flat enough

for wheelchairs most of the way. If it's crowded, visit the North Rim instead; it gets a tenth as many visitors as the South Rim, so there's rarely a crowd at parking lots, trailheads, or restaurants.

Climate change has already increased the number of days when it's simply too hot to descend much farther than Ooh-Aah Point, which is less than a mile (1.4 km) from the South Rim. Park officials have modeled what might happen if unusually hot days become the norm, or worse, if the region becomes as arid as the Sahara. In that scenario, entire forests could burn or die off, opening thousands of acres to invasive species. There's also an ongoing battle to keep uranium mines out of the Grand Canyon watershed. There are more than 600 claims on uranium near the canyon; without decisive action, those claims could become active mines, fouling groundwater for miles around.

Phoenix and Tucson

Enjoy these resort cities, in any season but summer.

"But it's a dry heat" has long been the rejoinder to complaints that the temperature in Arizona's desert cities is too hot. There's even some merit to that reasoning. A 90°F (32°C) day feels a lot more comfortable in Phoenix or Tucson than it does in Houston or even Boston, where those temperatures are often accompanied by sweltering humidity. If you're in the shade, anything under triple digits in Arizona is usually quite tolerable, and there's a lot to do.

More than 86% of Arizona's population lives in the Sun Corridor, which includes the cities of Phoenix and Tucson and their suburbs that sprawl

Plan Your Trip

Location: Southern Arizona

Getting There: Phoenix's Sky Harbor and Tucson International airports both receive flights from all over the U.S. and Canada; Phoenix also receives flights from a few European cities. The drive between the two cities takes about two hours.

When to Go: November to April.

like wildflowers across the Sonoran Desert. From November to April, days are bright and cloudless, perfect for golfing, hiking, playing tennis, horseback riding, or lounging poolside. Nights are cool and clear enough for stargazing.

Arizona's reputation as the spa capital of the world dates to the late 19th century, when thousands of tuberculosis patients moved to the southwest, hoping the dry air would cure the illness. Wellness is still the goal at today's spas, but treatments aim to remedy less-fatal maladies like aching bones or clogged pores. Scottsdale, a posh city northeast of central Phoenix, has more spas per capita than any U.S. city, usually ensconced within some of the ritziest resorts in the world.

More recently, Major League Baseball has been a major player in the population boom that made Phoenix the fastest growing major American city. The Arizona Diamondbacks joined the league as an expansion franchise in 1998; they're one of 15 major league teams that play their spring training games in Arizona's Cactus League, drawing fans from all over.

Unfortunately, temperatures the rest of the year may be the Sun Corridor's ultimate undoing. Tucson was the fifth-fastest-warming city in the country in 2021, with temperatures rising 4.6°F (2.6°C) since 1970. In Phoenix, the mercury has exceeded 115°F (46°C) just once a year on average since 1970, according to Climate Central. But if greenhouse gas emissions continue at their current rate, that temperature could be the norm for more than half the year by 2050. In that kind of heat, railroads can buckle, highways can melt, and the air becomes too thin for large planes to take off. What's worse, it won't even be a dry heat. Hotter temperatures are expected to bring higher humidity too, especially during the summer months, when sudden downpours create flash flooding—not to mention mosquitoes.

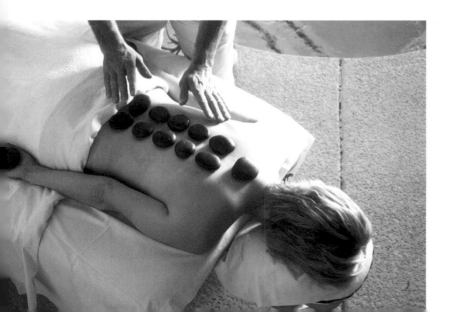

Glen Canyon National Recreation Area

One of America's most popular boating destinations might soon be better suited to hiking.

Since construction was completed in 1966, Glen Canyon Dam has been providing electricity and drinking water for a handful of western states and recreation opportunities to visitors from all over the Southwest. Behind the dam sits Lake Powell, the largest engineered lake in North America, with 1,960 miles (3,154 km) of shoreline spanning Arizona and Utah. Four marinas on the turquoise lake welcome boats of all kinds, especially houseboats, which are a Lake Powell standby because they require no special license to rent.

The lake's long, skinny shape lures water-skiers to its deep middle, while kayakers and canoers explore the numerous no-wake zones that branch off the main fork. Anglers often fish just below the dam, where the National Park Service offers an incentive of $25 (and at times, even more) for removing invasive brown trout longer than 6 inches (15 cm) from the lake. That's also the put-in point for many popular rafting trips, taking floaters through Horseshoe Bend, the most photographed location in the park. Swimming is permitted just about anywhere in the lake, but there are no lifeguards.

In the past few years, docks sitting on dry land hundreds of yards from water's edge have become a common sight, as the Southwest endures its worst drought in more than 1,200 years. In summer 2022,

Plan Your Trip

Location: Arizona and Utah

Getting There: The park is more or less equid stant from Las Vegas, Phoenix, and Salt Lake City, about four hours by car from each.

When to Go: The opportunity to jump into the lake and escape the scorching desert heat makes summer the most popular time of year to visit. Spring (March-May) and fall (Oct.-Dec.) are cooler but still warm enough for outdoor activities.

Lake Powell was just 24% full—the lowest it's ever been—with bathtub-style rings hundreds of feet high along the sandstone canyons reminding visitors where the water level used to be. The Bureau of Reclamation predicts that within the next five years, the water level could decrease to the point that the dam would cease to produce hydropower.

That's a disturbing trend for anyone who cares about the environment, and it's bad news for visitors looking for a water park in the middle of the desert. But not everyone is troubled by the disappearing lake, which has revealed buried treasures with every foot it recedes. Gregory Natural Bridge, for example,

one of the largest natural spans in the country, is no longer submerged underwater, but instead soars 20 feet above the surface. Whitewater rapids have returned to Cataract Canyon, a 46-mile (74-km) stretch of the lake that was too deep for such challenges before the drought. Coves that previously welcomed paddlers have become gorgeous red rock canyons beckoning hikers. Currently, the National Park Service does not maintain any trails in the recreation area, but that might change in the future, as Glen Canyon evolves from a water playground to a land-based attraction.

Yellowstone National Park

If you visit only one National Park in your lifetime, make it the world's first.

There's a reason Yellowstone was chosen as the world's first National Park back in 1872. It's the quintessential National Park. Just about anything you can imagine doing in a preserved wilderness environment, you can do in Yellowstone.

Like to spot big land animals? Yellowstone has 67 different mammal species, including black and grizzly bears, cougars, Canada lynx, gray wolves, and river otters. And those are just the carnivores. The list of ungulates includes moose, bighorn sheep, elk, mountain goats, pronghorns, and the literal show-stoppers: bison, who cross the roads in giant herds, causing the only traffic jams anybody is ever remotely happy to sit through.

How about birdwatching? Among the park's 285 different avian species are 19 types of raptors, including bald eagles, ospreys, peregrine falcons, American kestrels, and four different owl species; Yellowstone's wetlands attract Canada Geese and trumpeter swans.

Hiking? More than 900 miles (1,449 km) of trails range from the 0.6-mile (1.0-km) Trout Lake Trail to multi-day treks through untrammeled wilderness. There are hikes along the rim of a canyon, to the top of a mountain, around a lake, to a waterfall, along a creek—pretty much every kind of landscape

Plan Your Trip

Location: Northwest Wyoming and parts of Idaho and Montana

Getting There: Bozeman-Yellowstone International is the closest airport. The park is about a nine-hour drive from Denver.

When to Go: More than 80% of Yellowstone visitors arrive between June and September; almost a quarter of them in July. April, May, September, and October see significantly smaller crowds, although some roads may be closed.

you can think of. The 3-mile (5-km) trail from Chittenden Road to Mount Washburn takes you to the top of a 10,234-foot (3,122-meter) peak, with panoramic views up to 50 miles (80 km) away. Ten established bike trails welcome cyclists, while myriad lakes are open to canoeing, kayaking, and fishing. In winter, cross-country skiing, snowshoeing, and snowmobiling are the best ways to experience the relative solitude that descends when the summer crowds abate.

Prefer to see the sights without all the exertion? The 140-mile (230-km) Grand Loop Road links

Yellowstone's eight developed areas; a complete circuit takes up to seven hours without stops, but the stops are the point. The site almost everyone visits is Old Faithful, a geyser that erupts on average every 74 minutes, but it's merely the most famous of Yellowstone's cavalcade of thermal spectacles. People can hardly believe their eyes (or their selfies) when they see Grand Prismatic Spring. The largest hot spring in the U.S., it looks more like a lake painted by a rainbow. Mammoth Hot Springs, meanwhile, shows what happens when volcanically heated water seeps through limestone fractures and leaves behind travertine terraces as it cools. Elk love this part of the park.

A UNESCO World Heritage Site since 1978, Yellowstone faces threats to its existence that are as varied as its attractions. Invasive species pose a risk to its biodiversity. Forest fires grow bigger and hotter each year. There's also a remote threat of the big one: a massive volcanic eruption like the one that originally created this landscape more than two million years ago. A repeat of that prehistoric event is unlikely; more probable is an earthquake like the 7.3-magnitude tremor that occurred here in 1959. Yellowstone experiences up to 3,000 earthquakes a year, but most are too small to be felt.

Glacier National Park

The name might be a misnomer if you don't visit soon.

Read any story about the effects of climate change on America's national treasures, and you're bound to see mention of the irony of Glacier National Park losing its glaciers. During the previous decade, the National Park Service posted signs warning that the park's signature glaciers could be gone as early as 2020. That hasn't happened yet. But while the specific date of the glaciers' departure is now a bit more nebulous, there's no doubt that they are irrevocably shrinking. New signs now read: WHEN THEY WILL COMPLETELY DISAPPEAR DEPENDS ON HOW AND WHEN WE ACT.

Perhaps the greater irony, though, is that Glacier was never the best place for the average person to see glaciers. Most of the park's glaciers require a hike, often a strenuous one, and even then, they might be hard to distinguish from a plain old snowfield. (Two exceptions are the Jackson Glacier and the Salamander Glacier, both visible without leaving paved roads.) But while glaciers are what gave the park its name, the gorgeous landscape they have left behind is the real attraction.

Glacier encompasses more than a million acres (410,078 hectares) and nearly as many alpine lakes. There is essentially just one road through this unspoiled wilderness, and what a road it is! The Going-to-the-Sun Road is a narrow, winding ribbon of

blacktop through Glacier's five different ecosystems and habitat for 71 kinds of mammals (including mountain lions and wolverines) and 276 bird species. Even if you drive the entire 50-mile (80-km) length without leaving your car (and many visitors do exactly that), you'll be overwhelmed. The road itself is a remarkable accomplishment, with arches and tunnels carved by hand from the surrounding rock, enabling visitors to drive to vistas previously enjoyed only by bears, moose, bighorn sheep, and intrepid hikers. (Download the self-guided audio tour from the park website for more information about the road and what you'll see on either side of it.)

While Going to-the-Sun Road bisects the park east to west, the northernmost 110 miles (177 km) of the Continental Divide National Scenic Trail cleaves it north to south. Hundreds of people attempt to hike the trail's entire 3,059-mile (5,000-km) length between Mexico and Canada, but there are plenty of shorter routes within the park, including a 14-mile (23-km) round-trip outing to Triple Divide Peak, where water may flow east to Hudson Bay, south to the Gulf of Mexico, or west to the Columbia River.

Canada's Waterton Lakes National Park sits just across the border from Glacier; the two parks collectively comprise Waterton-Glacier International Peace Park, established in 1932. Wildlife routinely ranges across this solitary ecosystem unimpeded, but humans must still cross at a border checkpoint.

Plan Your Trip

Location: Northwest Montana

Getting There: The nearest major airports are Missoula International, about a three-hour drive south of the park, or Spokane International Airport in Washington, a beautiful five-hour drive away.

When to Go: Snow usually buries Going-to-the-Sun Road from mid-October through June (you can cross-country ski the road if it's closed to car traffic). From Memorial Day weekend to Labor Day, there is a $2 reservation ticket to drive the park's central artery.

Chicago

See what works in the "City That Works" … and what needs work.

Chicago works hard for its residents and visitors. This is a city that figured out how to jack up its buildings by several feet in order to install a public sewer system in the 1850s. It's a metropolis that rebuilt itself quickly after the famed 1871 fire that burned so many of those buildings to the ground. And it's a city that reversed the course of its namesake river to flush wastewater out of Lake Michigan, its main drinking water source. The river gets dyed green every year for St. Patrick's Day, and blue once a century, when the Cubs win the World Series. Architectural cruises along the river are an exceptional way to see the sights.

The Windy City has been welcoming visitors from around the globe ever since it took center stage at the World's Columbian Exposition of 1893. The fair, celebrating the 400th anniversary of Columbus's arrival in North America, transformed a town previously known for meatpacking into a global center of art, architecture, music, technology, food, and culture. Twenty-first-century additions to the landscape like Millennium Park's Pritzker Pavilion and Cloud Gate (a.k.a. the Bean) have attracted visitors to downtown Chicago in numbers too large for the city's founders to imagine.

Each spring, the city emerges from snow- and wind-induced hibernation and explodes into a riot of festivals reveling in Chicago's rich heritage.

Plan Your Trip

Location: Northeastern Illinois

Getting There: O'Hare International Airport receives passengers from 176 U.S. cities and 64 international destinations; smaller Midway International Airport is closer to downtown destinations.

When to Go: June, July, and August can be muggy. The shoulder seasons (April-May, October-November) have unpredictable weather, including the occasional rogue snowstorm.

Taste of Chicago, usually around July 4, serves up opportunities to sample menu items from some of the city's premier restaurants. It's also a chance to try classic local specialties like deep-dish pizza and Chicago-style hot dogs (with yellow mustard, relish, onions, tomatoes, pickle spears, celery salt, and sport peppers, but never ketchup), as well as some more international additions to the Chicago food scene.

Each week of the summer seemingly brings a festival of a different style: Blues Festival in June, Pitchfork Music Festival in July, country music and barbecue at the Windy City Smokeout in August, and JazzFest in September. Lollapalooza, a four-day

festival centered on alternative and punk rock, has called Chicago its permanent home since 2010. Chicago can also be an unexpected beach town, with 26 miles (40 km) of public sands, many with views of the skyscraper-filled skyline. Boats fill lakefront marinas and picnickers populate the parks and pastures along Lake Shore Drive.

In recent years, climate change has played havoc with the water level of Lake Michigan. As recently as 2013, it was at historic lows, fueling fears that it wouldn't be able to flush wastewater down the Chicago River. Seven years later, though, the lake was overflowing, wiping out sandy beaches and flooding homes and apartments near the coast. These huge oscillations have left city engineers scrambling to find a navigable course between the two extremes.

New Orleans

Join the party that never stops.

With apologies to Coolio, there ain't no party like a New Orleans party 'cause a New Orleans party truly doesn't stop. There's a reason the city has hosted the Super Bowl ten times (and will again in 2025). Simply put, New Orleans knows how to throw a bash. It has had nearly 200 years of experience staging the city's annual Mardi Gras blowout, and more than a century of practice tossing beads, doubloons, cups, and other worthless plastic trinkets from floats to the frenzied hands of spectators along the parade route. An amazing supply of brass marching bands seem to exist solely to maintain the party atmosphere between the floats.

Jazz Fest, the Big Easy's second-biggest annual fete, has only been around since 1970, but it too is suffused with everything that makes New Orleans wonderful. A dozen stages showcase some of the world's best musicians in a variety of styles, including jazz, blues, R&B, gospel, Cajun, zydeco, rock, rap, country, and bluegrass. The food at Jazzfest is equally endemic to New Orleans. Local vendors dish out jambalaya, alligator sausage, po' boys, muffulettas, crawfish, fried chicken, and countless other Louisiana specialties.

New Orleans's charms aren't limited to its two biggest annual events. The restaurant scene is

Plan Your Trip

Location: Southern Louisiana

Getting There: Louis Armstrong International Airport receives flights from London, Paris, and 50 North American cities.

When to Go: Anytime. There's always something going on in New Orleans, even in the dog days of August, when the weather is swampy. Mardi Gras (with official festivities and events throughout the two weeks leading up to Ash Wednesday) and JazzFest (the last weekend in April and first weekend in May) are the most popular (and expensive) times to visit.

unparalleled year-round. Every single meal is an occasion to sample something exceptional, be it oysters on the half shell, fine dining at one of the legendary heavyweights in the French Quarter, or coffee and beignets at Café du Monde. And you can burn off the calories dancing at any of the dozens of live music venues and clubs in the Faubourg Marigny.

Even funerals are festive in the birthplace of jazz. After solemn tributes to the departed, New

Orleans jazz funerals break out into singing and dancing (known as second lines), recognizing that life goes on and is a reason for celebration. So too is the gumbo of architectural styles in the French Quarter, Uptown, the Garden District, and other neighborhoods, each with their own unique look and feel.

Hurricanes—and not just the kind you drink—are a fact of life. Katrina nearly wiped the city off the map in 2005, as did Betsy before it in 1965. And while hundreds of thousands of people have since returned to New Orleans because they can't fathom living anywhere else, the city's population has never rebounded to pre-Katrina levels. Since 2005, existential threats to New Orleans have only increased, as rising global temperatures will lead to stronger hurricanes, more frequent floods, and more extreme heat waves.

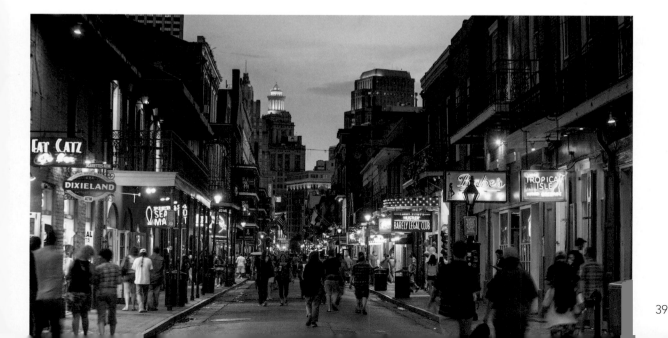

Miami

Splash in tropical turquoise waters before they get too close.

For Americans in the Northeast and Midwest, Miami looms almost as an apparition: an oasis of warmth, an escape valve for when the cold, dark days of winter become too intolerable to withstand. Flooded in sunlight and bathed in turquoise waters lapping tropical soft white sands, Miami has been welcoming snowbirds since the first Art Deco hotels went up in South Beach during the Depression. But the area didn't really capture America's fancy until the 1950s, when the Rat Pack made the Fontainebleau their winter playground, and Lucy and Desi Arnaz popularized Morris Lapidus's modernist Eden Roc hotel while filming episodes of "I Love Lucy" on location.

Meticulous restoration of those Art Deco buildings during the 1980s and 1990s birthed a second heyday for Miami, one that still draws

Bentleys and Maybachs to cruise the strip along Ocean Drive in search of the hottest nightlife. Partying all night and sleeping off a hangover on the beach the next day is as much a Miami institution as the Clevelander Hotel bar.

> ## Plan Your Trip
>
> **Location:** South Florida
>
> **Getting There:** Miami International Airport receives flights from all over the U.S. and dozens of cities in Latin America.
>
> **When to Go:** Avoid hurricane season (June-November). Even if a storm isn't brewing, afternoon rain showers are a near-daily event.

Like so many North Americans who originally flew south to escape winter, Cubans who fled to Miami to escape Fidel Castro's communist regime also decided to stay. Once known as the center of all things Cubano, Little Havana is now a hub of activity for residents and visitors of all backgrounds, especially during the Calle Ocho festival each spring. In 2017, Little Havana's multicultural population inspired the National Trust for Historic Preservation to declare the barrio a "national treasure," embodying the pursuit of the American dream. The city's overall population is still nearly three-quarters Latino, but it's not only Cubans. Immigrants from Guatemala, El Salvador, Nicaragua, Colombia, Venezuela, and Peru all contribute to this modern cosmopolitan city. Even as far south as Argentina, Miami is only half jokingly dubbed the capital of Latin America.

It should come as little surprise that Miami is in danger of disappearing. Most of the city sits no more than 6 feet (2 meters) above sea level. Hurricanes take aim at Florida every year, and about once a decade—Andrew in 1992, Wilma in 2005, Irma in 2017—a big one makes landfall and causes tens of billions of dollars in damages. The next Category 5 storm just might inundate South Florida once and for all—that is unless rising seas reclaim it a centimeter at a time first.

Florida Keys

Island hop by car or boat, for the time being.

There are more than 800 keys in this archipelago southwest of Miami, but the last in the chain, Key West, gets most of the attention—not to mention cruise ship traffic—in part due to its association with Ernest Hemingway. The Nobel Prize-winning author wrote several of his novels (including *A Farewell to Arms*) while living on the island; his home is now a museum open to the public and populated by dozens of six-toed cats. Hemingway was also a frequent guest at Sloppy Joe's bar, another Key West institution along touristy Duval Street that holds an annual "Papa" look-alike contest every July.

But while the end of the road has its appeals, the real allure of a Florida Keys vacation is the drive from Miami. Here is Florida on island time, attuned more to the tides than rush hour traffic. A single

Plan Your Trip

Location: South Florida

Getting There: Miami International Airport receives flights from all over the U.S. and dozens of cities in Latin America. There's also a regional airport in Key West from which you can fly back to the mainland if you don't want to drive.

When to Go: Avoid hurricane season (June-November). The Keys are usually a little bit warmer than Miami, and they get a little less rain. Don't come here for the beaches, though; most of the strands in the Keys are rocky, rather than sandy.

160-mile (257-km) thoroughfare—too low to the water to call it a highway—links the major keys like a charm bracelet, chained together by bridges and causeways. The most impressive of these is Seven-Mile Bridge, a 6.79-mile (11-km) span between Knight's Key and Little Duck Key that encompasses two separate structures: the Overseas Highway (a.k.a. Route 1), and the old railroad bridge parallel to it, which reopened in 2022 as a recreational path for biking, walking, and running in the middle of the Atlantic.

A driving tour of the keys usually begins in Miami, passing through Homestead, gateway to Everglades National Park. From there, the road jogs east to Key Largo, one of the best snorkeling destinations in America. Key Largo's John Pennekamp Coral Reef State Park was the first ever underwater state park. Its sheltered location and rich marine life make it a spectacular introduction for first-time snorkelers and divers.

Islamorada, about halfway to Key West, is often called the sportfishing capital of the world. This is the place to stop if you'd like to go out for big game fish like tarpon and sailfish, as well as smaller catch like bonefish and snook. If you'd rather feed the fish than have them feed you, stop at Robbie's Marina. Wherever you go, be sure to sample the Key Lime Pie. Everyone makes it a little differently: some firm like cheesecake, others airier like lemon meringue, but always with a sweetness and tartness that only comes from key limes. Green Turtle Inn in Islamorada wins raves for its entire menu, not just its desserts; you can't miss the big green neon turtle towering above the parking lot.

The Keys are even more vulnerable to sea-level rise than the rest of Florida. Average elevation here is just 3 feet (1 meter) above sea level, and if any of the bridges between the islands becomes submerged, there's no way out except by boat.

Savannah, Georgia

Experience Southern hospitality and food at its finest.

Don't go looking for Forrest Gump's bench on a visit to Savannah. You won't find it. The prop was removed from Chippewa Square after filming (although a replica is on display at the Savannah Visitors Center).

What you will find, however, is a genteel city draped in old Southern charm. Spanish moss hangs from live oak trees in the city's public parks and squares, while horse-drawn carriages clip-clop up and down cobblestone streets lined with antebellum buildings. Chippewa is one of 22 open squares or parks that checkerboard the orthogonal city center, meaning you're never more than a few blocks from a shady spot to people-watch. The squares are anchored by Forsyth Park, 30 acres (12 hectares) of greenery on the southern boundary of the city's historic district. The magnificent Forsyth Park Fountain, modeled after a similar fountain in Paris's Place de la Concorde, is one of Savannah's most-Instagrammed locations.

Savannah is renowned for its food—Southern food, that is. This is the place to go for classics like cornbread, hushpuppies, grits, and macaroni and cheese. When it comes to fried chicken, Mrs. Wilkes' Dining Room, Treylor Park, and the Olde Pink House are among the heavyweights that battle it out for the city's best version. Walk off those calories with a stroll down River Street, poking into shops that have taken up residence in former cotton

Plan Your Trip

Location: Eastern Georgia, near the South Carolina border

Getting There: Savannah Airport receives flights from more than a dozen cities east of the Rockies. Atlanta's much larger Hartsfield-Jackson International Airport is about a four-hour drive away.

When to Go: Spring (April-June) and fall (October-December) have the best weather, and smaller crowds than summer (July-September), which can be hot and muggy. Winter (January-March) is mild but typically not quite warm enough for outdoor dining.

warehouses. Bring your drinks with you, if you like; Savannah is one of the few cities that allow people to consume alcohol in public (in go-cups).

Savannah has been saved from destruction twice. After burning Atlanta and every other Confederate city he passed through on his 1864 "March to the Sea," Gen. William Tecumseh Sherman spared the city, and presented it to Abraham Lincoln as a Christmas gift. A century later, when many of downtown Savannah's stately prewar homes faced the wrecking ball because of decades of neglect, a group of women who later became the Historic Savannah Foundation raised funds to restore the

architectural gems one by one. Since 1960, the foundation has saved more than 400 buildings, and the Savannah Historic District, corresponding roughly to the pre-Civil War city limits, was named a National Historic Landmark District in 1966.

The next threat to Savannah, however, might be harder to overcome. The kind of massive floods that used to inundate the city once a century are becoming more frequent. Climatologists estimate that by 2050, the city could experience a so-called 100-year flood every year. As Forrest himself might have said, "you never know what you'll get." But it sure won't be a box of chocolates.

Charleston, South Carolina

Savor the subtle charms of the Low Country.

Charleston's appeal isn't immediately apparent. Church steeples, not tall buildings, dominate the skyline, hence the nickname "The Holy City." The metropolitan area is about the same size as Boise, Idaho, though it's South Carolina's largest city. It's on the Atlantic coast, but the nearest beaches are about 20 minutes away from downtown.

That's fine with the local residents, who are renowned for their friendliness, perhaps because of the laid-back pace of life. It's also fine with the millions of people who visit every year, including the readers of *Travel + Leisure* magazine, who named it the best city in the U.S. every year from 2013 to 2022, and best city in the world in 2016.

Some visitors come for the city's rich history. Cobblestones and bricks line the streets in the French Quarter, the core of historic Charleston. The landmark 1807 City Market still operates here,

Plan Your Trip

Location: Southeastern South Carolina

Getting There: Charleston International Airport is a misnomer, as there are no international flights to the city. The airport does, however, receive flights from dozens of cities across the U.S.

When to Go: Spring (March-May) and fall (September-November) have ideal weather: warm—but not hot—days, and cool—but not cold—nights. Airfares and hotel rates are usually highest during these peak seasons. Summer (June-August) can be hot and humid.

and the 1859 Old Slave Mart is now a museum that traces the history of trade in enslaved people. Heading south from the Quarter, Bay Street passes through an entire block of multi-hued

Georgian townhouses known as Rainbow Row before terminating at the Battery, a neighborhood of beautifully preserved antebellum mansions overlooking the water. Fort Sumter, where the first shots of the Civil War were fired in 1861, is a short ferry ride away.

Others come for the food, flavored by Charleston's waterfront location and by ingredients and recipes from Europe, West Africa, and the Caribbean. Local specialties include shrimp and grits, oysters, she-crab soup, hush puppies, or Frogmore Stew: a heaping platter of shrimp, smoked sausage, corn, and potatoes. But it's not all buttermilk biscuits and fried green tomatoes. Farm-to-table restaurants and James Beard Award-winners like FIG (Food is Good), Husk, and Rodney Scott's Whole Hog BBQ have made Charleston popular among foodies.

What the sea giveth, however, it also taketh away. This part of South Carolina is known as the low country, because so much of it sits on land less than 10 feet (3 meters) above sea level. But if sea level continues to rise at its current rate of ½ -inch (1.5 cm) per year, a good portion of Charleston could be underwater by century's end. Already, the number of days with tidal flooding has tripled since the 1990s. And while Charleston escaped serious damage during Hurricane Ian in 2022, it might not be so lucky as coastal storms grow more frequent and powerful.

North Carolina's Outer Banks

Enjoy beautiful beaches rich in history.

Renowned for its miles of gorgeous gold-sand dunes and beaches, this archipelago of barrier islands has been attracting visitors literally for centuries. For many families, the Outer Banks are a place to return year after year for quiet relaxation and a small-town environment that feels an ocean away from the mainland.

There is a surprising amount of history to explore here—and a stellar National Scenic Byway connecting the most popular stops. This 148-mile (238-km) system of two-lane roads, bridges,

Plan Your Trip

Location: Atlantic Ocean, parallel to the North Carolina coast

Getting There: The closest international airport is in Norfolk, VA, about a two-hour drive from the northernmost communities on the Outer Banks.

When to Go: Summer (June-August) is the most popular—and most expensive—season. But the water is warm enough for swimming in spring (April-June) and fall (September-November) and crowds and prices are lower than in high season.

and ferries is also known as North Carolina Highway 12, but it's too low and too pokey to be considered a true highway. That's in keeping with the laid-back nature of the territory it traverses.

At the northern end of the archipelago is Kill Devil Hills, where the Wright Brothers National Memorial commemorates the location of the first successful airplane flights in 1903. Boulders mark the spots where Orville took off and landed 120 feet (36 meters) away. Roanoke Island, just east of Nags Head, is the site of another landmark: Fort Raleigh, where the first English explorers arrived in 1584. The National Park Visitor Center tells the stories of the colonists, the Carolina Algonquians who preceded them, and the Freedmen's colony for formerly enslaved men and women established here in 1862.

Much of the land south of Nags Head looks a lot like it did to earlier generations of visitors, thanks to the Cape Hatteras National Seashore and the Pea Island National Wildlife Refuge, both of which have protected it from development. Cape Hatteras Light Station, the tallest (and possibly the most-photographed) brick lighthouse in the U.S., stands sentinel above one of the most hazardous sections of the Atlantic Coast.

The nearby Graveyard of the Atlantic Museum sheds light of a different kind on the 5,000-plus ships that have foundered in these treacherous waters over the last 500 years. Not surprisingly, this is a favored destination among scuba divers. The Outer Banks' herds of feral "banker ponies" are said to be descended from Spanish mustangs that swam to shore after one such shipwreck centuries ago. Other legendary vessels that have met their demise here include the ironclad USS *Monitor*, a key Union asset during the Civil War, and the *Queen Anne's Revenge*, which Edward Teach (a.k.a. the pirate Blackbeard) ran aground in 1718. Blackbeard was killed later that year in a dramatic battle on nearby Ocracoke Island, accessible today only by ferry.

For a place with so much history, the Outer Banks may not have much of a future. The islands are little more than spits of shifting sands that continually need refurbishment. Federal, state, and local governments spend millions of dollars replenishing beaches wracked by hurricanes every summer and Nor'easters every winter. Over the past decade or so, the Department of Transportation has spent half a billion dollars rebuilding Highway 12's bridges and most vulnerable sections of blacktop. And it may not be long before rising seas reclaim the islands entirely.

National Mall

Visiting now is a capital idea.

Walking the National Mall is a delightful way to experience the full scope of American history. Most of the wars the U.S. participated in are commemorated here in one way or another, from the site plan itself, commissioned by Revolutionary War hero George Washington, to the simple geometry of Maya Lin's Vietnam Veterans Memorial. Two of the three branches of government overlook the capital's central axis, and three of the four Mount Rushmore presidents (sorry, Teddy Roosevelt) are celebrated with imposing monuments or memorials.

Each generation of Americans has added its own stamp to the Mall, from the Washington Monument, whose construction was halted because of the Civil War, as well as the memorials to the two World Wars and the Korean War. The social history of the country unfurls here as well, starting with the inimitable 1885 Smithsonian "Castle." A statue of Dr. Martin Luther King Jr. stands a few hundred yards from the spot where he delivered his "I Have a Dream" speech to more than 200,000 civil rights demonstrators lining the Lincoln Memorial's reflecting pool.

Plan Your Trip

Location: Washington, D.C.

Getting There: Ronald Reagan Washington National Airport receives flights from all over the east coast. Transcontinental and international flights usually need the longer runways at Dulles International Airport.

When to Go: Summer (June-August) is the most popular time but can be sticky and hot, especially in August. Another busy season is the end of March or beginning of April, when the cherry trees blossom along the Jefferson Memorial's Tidal Basin.

Over the years, the Smithsonian's roster of museums—all of which are admission-free—has expanded to include the National Museum of American History (sometimes called the nation's attic for its collections celebrating all things uniquely American), the National Air and Space Museum, the National Portrait Gallery, the National Museum

of the American Indian, and the National Museum of African American History and Culture. And plans are underway for the National Museum of the American Latino and the Smithsonian American Women's History Museum.

Despite all the new arrivals over the years, the 156-acre (63-hectare) site still feels boundless,

integrating each new landmark into the fabric of the nation. Lawns and other shady spaces give the entire site a park-like feel, with plenty of places for quiet relaxation or sipping a lemonade while recharging your feet.

Much of the National Mall (not to mention huge swaths of the capital) was originally built on marshland reclaimed from Chesapeake Bay, land that's now subsiding while the surrounding rivers and estuaries are rising at a rate twice the national average. By 2100, Washington will suffer from more floods than it already does, and some forecasts predict large sections of the Mall will be completely underwater. Maybe even more dire is how a warmer planet will affect the cherry trees along the Jefferson Memorial: they likely won't blossom at all without at least a month of temperatures below 41°F (5°C).

New York City

Don't sleep on the city that never stops.

New York is often called the "City That Never Sleeps" because there are so many things going on after sunset. The subway runs all night, many bars don't close until 4 AM, and restaurant kitchens stay open late to welcome diners after a Broadway show, a Soho gallery opening, a concert at Carnegie Hall, or a movie premiere.

But the nickname also acknowledges the fact that New York never stops. The only constant in Gotham is change. If you haven't been to New York in a while, you might not recognize it. After seven years, *Hamilton* is no longer the toughest ticket on Broadway (although it's still not easy to find seats most nights). Lincoln Center's Avery Fisher Hall has been renamed for David Geffen, with promises that its dreadful acoustics have been rehabilitated. The Empire State Building is now the city's seventh-tallest edifice, surpassed in the last decade by new glass and steel towers. At least a half dozen other skyline-altering projects are already in the works. And two transportation developments—the Citi Bike bicycle-sharing program and the Second

Avenue subway—have made it slightly easier to get around traffic-choked Manhattan.

Of course, some things about New York never change, not even after a global pandemic. Most New Yorkers are still friendly, their reputation for rudeness notwithstanding. Ellis Island is still more interesting than the Statue of Liberty. Walking across the Brooklyn Bridge still inspires awe. The Metropolitan

Plan Your Trip

Location: Southern New York

Getting There: The New York City metropolitan area is home to three of the world's largest airports: John F. Kennedy International, LaGuardia, and Newark Liberty International across the Hudson River in New Jersey.

When to Go: Anytime, but the best weather for walking around the city is in May to June and September to October. The holiday season (between Thanksgiving and New Year's Day) is an especially popular time to visit.

Museum steps are still a great place to meet people—or just people-watch—on a warm spring day. *Chicago*, *The Lion King*, and *Wicked* still play to packed houses after more than 7,000 performances each, though *Phantom of the Opera* was set to end its historic 35-year run in 2023. And the Knicks are still terrible at basketball, even according to their biggest fans.

In coming years, the Big Apple is likely to see some changes of a more troubling nature, as sea level rises, shorelines erode, coastal storms become more frequent and intense, and the asphalt jungle makes heat waves even hotter. New York got a taste of this future in 2012, when Hurricane Sandy inundated subway stations and knocked out power to millions of residents. Battery Park City and other neighborhoods erected on landfill weren't built to withstand 100-year floods that are now expected once a decade. Warmer winters will also lengthen breeding seasons for ticks and mosquitoes, increasing incidence of Lyme disease and West Nile virus throughout the five boroughs.

Alaska

Experience the Last Frontier's natural wonders … while they last.

They don't call Alaska the Last Frontier for nothing. Twice as large as Texas, the 49th state is approximately one-fifth the size of the first 48, with more coastline than the rest of the U.S. combined. Here is a land of few people and even fewer roads, but more than 3 million lakes, 100,000 glaciers, 3,000 rivers, and 130 volcanoes. The state is home to the country's two largest national forests, 17 of the 20 highest mountain peaks, and 8 national parks, none of which see more than 700,000 visitors a year (Yosemite, by contrast, gets nearly 5 million).

The Inside Passage, a labyrinth of islands, straits, and sounds between Washington and mainland Alaska, is a favorite of cruise ships. Shore excursions here might include whale-watching, dogsledding, fishing for salmon, river-rafting through bald eagle habitat, or following in the footsteps of 1897-1898 Klondike gold rush prospectors. Bus-sized chunks of blue ice calve into the fjords below at Glacier Bay National Park and Preserve, another unforgettable Inside Passage highlight.

At the opposite end of the state, the Bering Land Bridge National Preserve safeguards the remains of a corridor that connected Asia and North America 13,000 years ago. The Aleutian Islands, an archipelago in Alaska's southwest corner, span the 180th meridian dividing the world's two hemispheres, so they technically include both the

Plan Your Trip

Location: West of British Columbia and the Yukon Territory

Getting There: Ted Stevens Anchorage International airport receives flights from more than a dozen U.S. cities and summer-only service from Frankfurt, Germany. Cruises of the Inside Passage usually depart from Seattle or from Ketchikan, Alaska.

When to Go: Summers (June-August) are short this far north, but they make up for it with long days and short nights. In some parts of the state, the sun doesn't set between May and July. This is by far the most popular time to visit.

westernmost and easternmost points in the U.S. The northern latitude and remote location make Alaska ideal for viewing the Aurora Borealis.

Halfway between coastal Anchorage and remote Fairbanks, Denali National Park is home to North America's tallest mountain. The park is also a pretty good metaphor for the entire state. Unlike other national parks, Denali is intentionally undeveloped, designed to protect a primitive wilderness and the wildlife within it. Among the 39 species of mammals found here are the Alaskan "big five": moose,

caribou, Dall sheep, grizzly bears, and wolves. There are only a handful of marked trails in the park, and the lone road is off-limits to private vehicles (buses ferry visitors to the park's outer reaches).

Alaska is the fastest-warming state in the country, and climate change is already marring much of its enduring appeal. Its glaciers are melting at record pace, and the amount of sea ice is only half of what existed 40 years ago. In 2022, the state canceled snow crab fishing season for the first time ever because the Bering Sea water was too warm. Thawing permafrost below the earth's surface creates subsidence, cracking and buckling any roads atop it, including the one through Denali, which has been closed multiple times over the past decade due to cave-ins. Longer, drier summers have also sparked more wildfires than in any decade since Alaska became a state.

Hawai'i

Soak up America's island paradise.

Hawaii has been a U.S. state for more than 60 years, but in many ways, it remains a territory all its own. English is the official language of the islands, but so is Hawaiian, a mellifluous tongue with only eight consonants, plus a glottal stop (denoted by a ') that puzzles many newcomers. Visitors from the lower 48 don't need to carry a passport or exchange currency, but there are plenty of tourists from the Far East

who do. Hawaii is actually closer to Tokyo than it is to New York, and the Asian influence is palpable throughout the islands of aloha.

Everyone knows Hawaii is a tropical paradise, the birthplace of modern surfing, land of luaus and hula dancing, and a place where it's perfectly appropriate to wear flip-flops and a brightly colored floral shirt to all but the most formal occasions. Luxury hotels line the shores of all the major islands, but there are still plenty of mom-and-pop operations, and even some undeveloped coastline so rugged that movie directors have used it as a setting for mythical places like Jurassic Park and Neverland.

Oahu is the most urbanized of the islands, home to the capital, Honolulu, and world-famous Waikiki Beach. Kauai is the sleepiest, carpeted in palm trees and waterfalls and stunningly secluded beaches. The Big Island is home to active volcanoes, some of the most world's luxurious beachfront resorts, cowboy country, and the annual Ironman Triathlon. Maui is a veritable pu pu platter of all the islands, combining the sophisticated dining and nightlife (and traffic) of Oahu, the tranquility of Kauai, and the volcanic terrain (minus the actively flowing lava) of the Big Island.

All four major islands are ringed by gorgeous beaches (in shades ranging from talcum-powder white to volcanic black, from garnet red to olive green) and coral reefs that attract turtles, dolphins, tropical fish, and snorkelers. Those attractions are threatened by warmer temperatures and rising seas. A 2020 report by ProPublica found that Oahu, Maui, and Kauai had lost a quarter of their beaches over the past century. In 2021, Hawaii became the first U.S. state to declare a climate emergency. The legislation formally acknowledges the impending disaster posed by climate change and commits the state to a fully renewable energy grid by 2045.

Plan Your Trip

Location: Pacific Ocean

Getting There: All four major islands receive nonstop flights from the mainland, including some from the east coast.

When to Go: Hawaii enjoys tropical weather year-round, but summer (June-August) tends to be hotter and more humid than the rest of the year. November-April is the rainy season; during these months, the south and west coasts of each island are more reliably sunny than the north and east coasts. Airfares are highest in the last two weeks of December. May is spectacular.

Volcanoes National Park

If you're not careful, lava might get to it before you do.

Volcanoes National Park isn't only one of the most unique installations in the National Park System. It just might be the most unique place in the entire United States. Nowhere else will you see actively erupting lava flowing down the side of a mountain. No wonder it's been a UNESCO World Heritage Site since 1987.

You needn't worry about being swept up in a fiery hot cascade of molten rock or choking on ash. Unlike composite volcanoes, which explode all at once (think Vesuvius), Hawaii's volcanoes are shield volcanoes, which bubble and ooze lava slowly enough for visitors to give it a wide berth. Technically there are two active volcanoes in the park: Mauna Loa,

Plan Your Trip

Location: Big Island of Hawai'i

Getting There: The closest airport is in Hilo, about 45 minutes away by car. Kona International Airport, on the west side of the island, is about two hours away by car. Many visitors prefer to stay on the Kona side of the island because Hilo is the rainiest city in America.

When to Go: Almost any time of year is a good time to visit. The volcano area doesn't get as much rain as Hilo, but it can be hot in summer. Airfares and hotel rates are highest in December and around Easter.

which erupted in 2022 for the first time in nearly 40 years, and Kilauea, which has hardly stopped since 1983. Kilauea's eruptions are constantly changing the national park's dimensions, forcing rangers to figure out where to safely send visitors almost daily.

The park's website and app frequently update the premier places to see lava streams, steam venting from cracks in the ground, and of course the simmering cauldron. As of summer 2022, the best viewing was at three locations around the Kilauea Caldera: Uekahuna, on the northwest side; Keanakako'i, on the southeast side, and Kupina'i Pali (a.k.a. Waldron Ledge), closest to the Visitor Center, yet oddly the least crowded. All three viewpoints require a short walk over even terrain.

Hot flowing lava is of course the highlight of the park, but it isn't the only reason to visit Volcanoes. The path lava leaves behind as it cools creates a unique and eerie landscape. The 3.3-mile (5.3-km) hiking trail across the floor of Kilauea Iki Crater is surprisingly serene, a stunning contrast to its state in 1959, when it was a lake of boiling lava. The Thurston Lava Tube (Nahuku) was once a river of underground lava; today it's a mile-long (1.6-km) tunnel, especially popular on hot days.

The 19-mile (31-km) Chain of Craters Road is a memorable driving tour, a serpentine route past half a dozen previous eruption sites, ending at the ocean, where a 1983 eruption reclaimed the road. From there, you can walk about 1,000 feet (305 meters) across hardened smooth lava to the Holei Sea Arch, a tunnel-like formation created by lava pouring into the ocean and then eroding.

If the lava is coursing into the ocean during your visit, you can watch from the safety of a boat. Note that only operators with Coast Guard approval can get within 984 feet (300 meters) of actively flowing lava. Helicopter tours are an unforgettable (albeit expensive) way to fly over the bubbling cauldron. Many helicopter tours also fly over hidden valleys and waterfalls visible only from the air.

Route 66

Get your kicks where and while you can.

One of the first highways in the United States, Route 66 opened in 1926, linking Chicago to Los Angeles and accelerating a great migration of Americans west to California's sunny shores. Immortalized by a 1946 song and a 1960s TV show, the 2,448-mile (3,940-km) road symbolized American mobility and opportunities for a fresh start like no other thoroughfare had before—or since.

Even in its earliest days, the route was constantly being modified as traffic increased, bypassing smaller towns in the name of speed. But it remained contiguous until 1956, when the Interstate Highway System began to render it obsolete. Over the next 29 years, one state after another decertified portions of the "Main Street of America," and in 1985, it was decommissioned as a U.S. route. Big patches of the so-called Mother Road remained intact, however, and from 1985 and 1990, organizations in Illinois, Missouri, Kansas, Oklahoma, Texas, New Mexico, Arizona, and California sprang up to preserve the remnants.

Since 1999, the National Park Service has coordinated those efforts in the Route 66 Corridor Preservation Program. HISTORIC ROUTE 66 signs mark the road's starting point in Chicago, the western terminus in Santa Monica, and hundreds of other historic places and curiosities in between. Attractions along the way include motels and drive-in theaters frozen in time when the interstate highway bypassed their little towns, beautifully restored diners in small cities where there's still enough traffic to support these small businesses, the Gateway Arch in St. Louis, and Cadillac Ranch in Amarillo, Texas.

The Park Service website lists more than 100 restored historic districts, bridges, gas stations, theaters, and trading posts worth a stop along the way. Several private organizations have already done the legwork of piecing them together on a map that you can use to navigate a scenic driving tour. There

Plan Your Trip

Location: Chicago to Los Angeles, passing through six other states along the way.

Getting There: Chicago and Los Angeles have two of the biggest airports in the world.

When to Go: Anytime.

are long stretches where the re-created route overlaps a charmless interstate highway, as well as sections that poke along through tiny hamlets.

To see the sights at a more leisurely pace, cycle the sections in Missouri, Kansas, Oklahoma, and California that have been deemed part of U.S. Bicycle Route 66. It's not a dedicated bike path, so some of the route overlaps busy roads. But the designated sections feature road signs that say 66 with a bicycle icon.

Chinatown

It's a great place to visit, but an increasingly expensive place to live.

Originally shaped by people forbidden from living anywhere else, ethnic Chinese neighborhoods across America quickly became vital parts of the urban fabric in many cities. In addition to serving as a place where Chinese Americans could live and own businesses, Chinatowns created communities where new immigrants could read the street signs, find reminders of home, and learn the ins and outs of their adopted country from previous generations.

People of non-Asian descent also came to value Chinatowns for their authentic restaurants—not just Cantonese, but Hunan, Szechuan, and other regional specialties—as well for shops selling inexpensive seafood and fresh vegetables that weren't yet supermarket staples. And in many cities, Lunar New Year celebrations were a prime attraction for people of all ancestries.

The oldest—and still one of the largest—Chinatowns in North America is in San Francisco.

Plan Your Trip

Location: Major metropolitan areas across the United States

Getting There: Take the subway or bus, if there is one. Urban centers often have limited street parking.

When to Go: Anytime.

It dates to the latter half of the 19th century, when construction of the Transcontinental Railroad required significant immigrant labor. In the 21st century, however, Chinatowns are beginning to shrink, diversify, and in many cases disappear. A 2013 study by the Asian-American Legal Defense and Education Fund found that Asians were no longer a majority of the residents

in the Chinatowns of Boston, New York, and Philadelphia, and the Chinese population of Washington, D.C.'s Chinatown was just 300, a tenth of what it once was.

Part of the diaspora can be attributed to the American Dream. As they prospered, Asian Americans moved on to leafier neighborhoods, dispersing beyond dense first-generation enclaves just as other immigrant groups have done. Gentrification has also played a part. Neighborhoods once considered the outskirts have become prime urban real estate, with rents too high for new immigrants or even some long-time residents.

This development isn't entirely negative. In many U.S. cities, Chinese populations haven't dwindled; they've just moved where the cost of living is lower. New York City's Manhattan Chinatown, for example, is still home to the largest concentration of Chinese residents in the Western Hemisphere. But there are now at least eight other mini-Chinatowns in the city's other four boroughs, and three more in New Jersey.

Banff National Park

See what glaciers can do to alpine lakes … as long as there are still glaciers.

Canada's first national park is also its most popular, drawing more than 4 million visitors to the Rocky Mountains every year. Few leave disappointed. The scenery is simply jaw-dropping, particularly the numerous alpine lakes, whose teal blue color is like nothing else. Lake Louise gets by far the most attention, thanks in part to the majestic hotel that overlooks it. But Banff is full of smaller, less-visited lakes where silt known as glacial flour creates the otherworldly hue.

The 150-car parking lot at Moraine Lake, for example, keeps crowds to a minimum, and even the shuttle bus fills up quickly. Bow Lake and Peyto Lake are two of the most popular stops along the Icefield Parkway, which connects Banff to adjacent Jasper National Park. But most visitors come and go quickly in their quest to see waterfalls farther north or walk atop the Athabasca Glacier. Lake Minnewanka and its little brother Two Jack Lake, at the southeastern corner of the park, are even closer

to downtown Banff—maybe even walking distance for fit hikers. Scuba divers willing to brave icy waters can dive down to Minnewanka Landing, the original town here that was flooded by a dam in 1942.

Wildlife is everywhere in Banff, and the 30-mile (48-km) Bow Valley Parkway, which parallels the Trans-Canada Highway, is indeed the scenic route. It's a favorite among cyclists, and often visited by

> ## Plan Your Trip
>
> **Location:** Western Alberta, Canada
>
> **Getting There:** Banff is about a 90-minute drive from Calgary International Airport or a four-hour drive from Edmonton International Airport.
>
> **When to Go:** Summer (June-August) is the most popular time of year, followed by winter (December-February), when hiking up the Rockies gives way to skiing down them.

moose, deer, and other large land mammals. Elk number in the thousands and occasionally wander into the town of Banff to munch on residents' lawns. You'll hear them before you see them during the fall rutting season, when males bugle to attract mates. Bighorn sheep tend to stay at higher elevations but are often visible at the top of the Sulphur Mountain gondola. Black bears (which can be brown, black,

or beige) are often visible on the Trans-Canada Highway. Grizzlies outnumber brown bears in the park, but they're much more elusive.

Ospreys haunt the rivers and lakes, where they return to the same nest every spring and summer. Unless a Canada goose gets there first, that is. Look for bald eagles high in the sky above the intersection of meadows and bodies of water. Dawn and dusk are usually the best times to spot wildlife.

Climatologists predict that climate change will have an especially poignant effect on Banff, Jasper, and five other national parks in the Rockies. As temperatures rise over the next 50 years, even more glaciers will melt away until there's no glacial flour left to give the lakes their unique color. What's worse, nitrogen from air pollution and phosphorus from wildfires are already turning the water green, rather than blue.

Churchill, Manitoba

Visit polar bears on their home turf while the Great White North is still cold enough.

There are bears, and then there are *polar* bears. Bears are found throughout North and South America, Europe, and Asia. Polar bears, on the other hand, live exclusively in the Arctic, in territory belonging to just five countries: the U.S. (Alaska), Russia, Norway, Denmark (Greenland), and Canada, which is home to about 60% of all polar bears.

The southernmost polar bear habitat is near tiny Churchill, Manitoba, where the world's largest bears often outnumber the human residents, earning it the nickname "The Polar Bear Capital of the World." Churchill is one of the easiest places to view the carnivores, although "easy" is somewhat relative. There are no roads to Churchill, so the only way to get there is by plane or train. The train ride crosses through the boreal forest on its way to the arctic tundra; the flight from Winnipeg delivers splendid aerial views of Hudson Bay.

Each October, as the weather turns colder, hundreds of polar bears make their way to the shores of Hudson Bay, looking to catch a ride on a sheet of sea ice to deeper waters, where they can hunt for

Plan Your Trip

Location: Northernmost Manitoba, Canada

Getting There: The closest major airport is Winnipeg International, where several airlines connect to Churchill; the flight is about 90 minutes. Trains depart from Winnipeg every Tuesday and Saturday for the 48-hour trip to Churchill.

When to Go: October is the prime month for polar bear viewing. The world's greatest concentration of Beluga whales—up to 60,000 of them—migrate across Hudson Bay between June and September, but bear sightings are uncommon this time of year.

ringed seals, their favorite prey. For most visitors, that's the optimum time to visit. A handful of operators offer tours of the area in so-called tundra buggies, buses equipped with oversized wheels for driving on snow and ice, and an enclosed, elevated platform that keeps visitors safe from curious bears who often come right up to the vehicles.

A lucky few, however, journey here in February or March, denning season for polar bear cubs and their mothers. Wat'chee Expeditions is the only outfitter authorized to take visitors into nearby Wapusk National Park, where they can come as close as 100 meters (328 feet) from the bears. At this chilly time of year, visitors might also see wolves, caribou, and arctic foxes.

Sadly, climate change has shortened the polar bears' feeding season by about 12 days in the past decade, because sea ice is forming later in the fall and breaking up earlier in the spring. Polar bears survive on fat stores between spring and fall, conserving their energy for the hunting season ahead. But starvation starts to set in if they go for more than 180 days without a seal meal. Polar bear populations in Hudson Bay have dropped 30% since 1987, and Polar Bears International expects that almost all polar bears will be gone by the end of this century.

Toronto

Explore Canada's city of neighborhoods before they're inundated.

Canada's biggest and most multicultural city is also its most-visited destination. The friendly local population welcomes 27 million people to the shores of Lake Ontario every year, more than Montréal and Vancouver combined.

Since it opened in 1976, CN Tower has dominated the Toronto skyline. Soaring 1,815 feet (553 meters) into the air, it's the tallest structure in the Western Hemisphere. Visitors can walk atop the glass floor at the Main Observation Level (1,136 feet/346 meters) or ascend the length of another football field to Skypod, where they can feel the building sway in the wind. Daredevils can circumnavigate the outside—you heard right!—of the observation level like Spiderman, secured only by a climbing harness.

Plan Your Trip

Location: Southeastern Ontario, Canada

Getting There: Toronto's Lester Pearson International Airport receives flights from five continents (sorry, Australia).

When to Go: Summer (June-August) is high season, both for temperatures and hotel prices. Both are lower in May and September, which can occasionally be downright chilly.

The other defining feature of Toronto's skyline is Rogers Centre. Known as Skydome when it opened in 1989, it was the first stadium with a fully retractable roof. It's no longer state-of-the-art, but

if the roof is open, it's still an appealing place to catch a baseball game. For the best views of the full skyline, catch a ferry to the Toronto Islands just a short distance into Lake Ontario, but a world away from the hubbub of the city. The ideal skyline views are at sunset, but you can spend the entire day at the beach or the Centreville Amusement Park, then nab the best snapshots.

Toronto is often described as a city of neighborhoods, in large part because so many of the towns and villages that have been incorporated into the city still retain their individual character. The world-renowned St. Lawrence Market makes Old Town a draw for foodies. Greek tabernas line the sidewalks on Danforth Street. Queen Street West used to be the hippest corner of the city; that distinction now perhaps belongs to Ossington Avenue. A thriving Chinatown abuts Kensington

Market, whose colorful shops and restaurants make it one of the city's most-photographed neighborhoods.

If you think you can escape the effects of global warming simply by migrating to cool Canada, think again. Temperatures are warming twice as fast in Canada as they are in the rest of the world, a trend that is already bringing more extreme heat waves—not to mention ticks and mosquitoes—to a country without a lot of air conditioners. Winters might become a little balmier, but if even half of the 47 inches (118 cm) of snow that falls on Toronto every year comes in the form of rain, it won't just make local ponds unplayable for hockey. All that water needs to go somewhere, which means flooding of Lake Ontario and the rivers that feed it.

The *Titanic*

Take a deep dive to the wreckage; its heart might not go on forever.

For more than 70 years after the RMS *Titanic* crashed into an iceberg on its maiden voyage, its location at the bottom of the Atlantic remained a mystery. But since the wreck was discovered in 1985, it has been visited by numerous expeditions, and more than 5,000 artifacts—including White Star Line china, portholes, pocket watches stopped at the time of the sinking, dishes, and the violin that bandleader Wallace Hartley continued to play as the ship sank—have been salvaged and sold at auction.

Plundering of the ship's treasure trove of souvenirs came to an end on the 100th anniversary of the shipwreck in 2012, when it became eligible for UNESCO's Convention on the Protection of Underwater Cultural Heritage. And in 2021, Ocean Gate Expeditions started offering space on its five-member submersibles to the public. The excursion isn't cheap: the company charges

Plan Your Trip

Location: North Atlantic Ocean. Expeditions leave from St. John's, Newfoundland.

Getting There: St. John's receives direct flights from half a dozen Canadian cities, and from Orlando, FL.

When to Go: For expedition dates, you must apply to become a mission specialist.

$250,000 to train and transport newbie "mission specialists" 12,800 feet (3,800 meters) to the ocean floor. In addition to the pilot, each crew includes a content specialist (usually a marine biologist, *Titanic* historian, microbiologist, or other expert) to help participants understand what they're seeing.

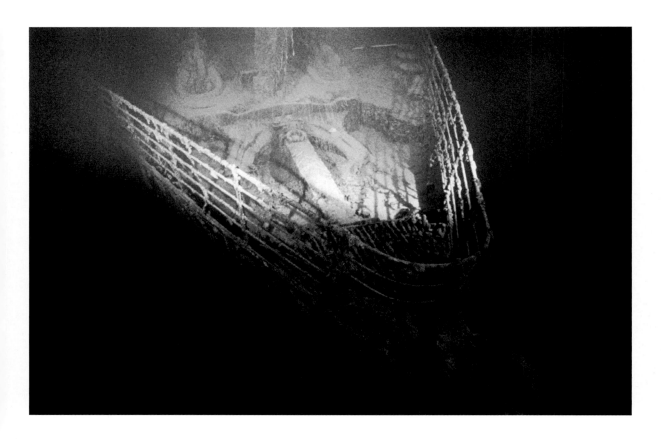

The eight-day expeditions leave from St. John's, Newfoundland, and include one dive to the wreck as well as accommodations and all meals on the support ship. The company supplies all the necessary gear, but participants must be 18 years or older and be able to climb ladders and carry 20 pounds. The voyage between the support ship and the wreck lasts about 2.5 hours each way, leaving about three hours to explore the ruins over the 8-10-hour expedition. And yes, there's a bathroom on the submersible. A small portable one, but a toilet, nonetheless.

Although seawater has done a pretty good job of preserving the extant portions of the *Titanic*, it isn't invulnerable to the elements. Corrosion, ocean currents, and newly discovered species of iron-eating bacteria known as *halomonas titanicae* threaten the integrity of the wreck. Some experts predict that the ship will disintegrate completely within the next 30 years.

Mexico City

Enjoy incredible art, food, and architecture before one of the world's great cities sinks.

Twenty million Mexicans can't be wrong. That's approximately how many people have migrated to Mexico City in the past 70 years, expanding the city's footprint 100-fold into the sprawling megalopolis it is today. But while so many locals were drawn to the capital by the prospect of employment, the cosmopolitan city they've created is even more appealing for visitors.

History is everywhere in the Distrito Federal (or DF, for short), especially in the Zócalo, or central public square. The ancient ruins of the Aztecs' Templo Mayor stand shoulder to shoulder with the Metropolitan Cathedral, built by Spanish colonists between 1573 and 1813. Tlatelolco, a more intact Aztec ruin, is the centerpiece of the 1966 Plaza de las Tres Culturas, which celebrates Mexico's history from pre-Columbian times through colonization up to independence.

Art is equally ubiquitous, not only in the 180+ museums—Mexico City has more museums than any city outside London—but also on a myriad of murals painted on the sides of buildings. Some of the best public art is concentrated in the La Roma neighborhood, which is a pleasant place for an afternoon stroll. Or head straight to the Palacio de Bellas Artes, whose walls are adorned with oversized works by Diego Rivera, José Clemente Orozco, and David Alfaro Siqueiros. Another Rivera mural climbs the stairs inside the Palacio Nacional as it chronicles eight centuries of Mexican history.

Architecture aficionados head straight for Paseo de la Reforma, Mexico's answer to the Champs-Élysées. Several of the city's most recognizable landmarks line this wide, leafy boulevard, including the Angel of Independence Fountain and the Art Deco-style Lotería Nacional building. Walk north to south to end up at Bosque de Chapultepec, an enormous city park with a zoo and even

Plan Your Trip

Location: Central Mexico

Getting There: Mexico City International Airport receives flights from more than 100 cities in 24 countries worldwide, including more than two dozen in the U.S.

When to Go: Spring (March-May) offers the best combination of warm and dry weather. Winters at this elevation (7,872 feet/2,400 meters) can be cold, and summers hot and rainy.

more museums scattered across its 1,700 acres (687 hectares).

Throughout the city, you'll see buildings that undulate or lean, telling the capital's geological history. The Aztecs founded Tenochtitlan in 1325 on an island in a series of lakes and canals. You can still see the vestiges of this ancient history in the Xochimilco neighborhood, a UNESCO World Heritage site where brightly colored boats called *trajineras* ply the extant canals, often accompanied by mariachis. The Spanish, however, drained the lakes and dumped landfill atop soft clay soil, which is sinking fast—in some areas up to 9 inches (23 cm) annually! As the population continues to grow, so too does the demand for water, forcing city officials to drill deeper into the aquifers (exacerbating the subsidence) or import it at astronomical expense.

CENTRAL AMERICA

AND THE **CARIBBEAN**

Bahamas

Get away without going far away.

The Bahamas are less than a half-hour flight from Miami, but they are a world away from life on the mainland. It's no exaggeration to say you could spend your entire vacation coming up with names to describe the cream-swirled azure waters on the islands where Christopher Columbus first made landfall in 1492. Is this beach teal or aqua? Are those shallows emerald or jade? The deep indigo of sapphire, or a richer cerulean? The ice-blue of Windex, or the turquoise of Scope?

The list of things to do in The Bahamas is as long as its roster of islands, cays, and atolls: more than 700 of them in total. White sand beaches are a given on most of the islands, except on Eleuthera, where they're pink, the product of microorganisms from nearby reefs washing ashore. Swimming with pigs, on the other hand, is an unexpected thrill on Big Major Cay, one of the 365 islands in Exuma. You can even feed them (pit-free fruits and vegetables only, please). In the shallow waters around nearby Bock Cay, you can strap on a mask and scoop conchs off the sea floor. Conchs are so abundant

Plan Your Trip

Location: Atlantic Ocean. Geographically, The Bahamas (and the Turks and Caicos Islands) are outside the boundaries of the Caribbean Sea. But politically, they are aligned with the islands and Central American states (Belize, Guyana, Suriname) of the Caribbean community.

Getting There: Major U.S. airlines have nonstop flights to Nassau from more than a dozen North American cities, and some have direct service to the Out Islands as well.

When to Go: Avoid hurricane season (usually May-November). Rates are highest in December, early January, mid-February, and March. April is the perfect combination of warm, dry weather, and smaller crowds.

(just try and find a local menu that doesn't boast conch fritters or chowder) they've even been used as building materials.

As impressive as they are from shore, the waters are perhaps even more transfixing from a boat. Whether you charter your own sailboat around the Out Islands, go sportfishing in the Biminis, take a snorkeling cruise from your Nassau hotel, or just rent a wave runner for a few hours, getting out on the water should figure prominently in your plans. The best snorkeling and diving is along the 140-mile (225-km) Andros Island Reef, which attracts seahorses, rays, turtles, and all manner of tropical fish. Or off Grand Bahama, where Theo's Wreck, the remains of a 262-foot (80-meter) freighter, decays in the warm water.

Most of The Bahamas' landmass—and 90% of its freshwater stores—sits no more than 5 feet (1.5 meters) above the waterline, making sea level rise the most immediate threat to the nation's future. Unless hurricanes flatten it first, that is. In 2019, Hurricane Dorian thrashed the archipelago with 185-mph (298 kmph) winds. It was the strongest storm ever recorded in The Bahamas, killing 74 people and destroying the main airport terminal on Grand Bahama. Visitors today therefore not only enjoy a memorable vacation; they help a nation dependent on tourism rebound from its toughest blow.

Cuba

Go before the political situation changes ... there or here.

Yes, you can travel to Cuba. But it's a little complicated. And the rules for visiting change frequently, depending on which political party occupies the White House. That said, as of 2022, Americans are free to fly directly to Cuba from five different U.S. gateways, as long as the purpose of their visit falls into one of 12 approved categories. This list includes religious activities, humanitarian aid, family visits, educational exchanges, and the somewhat vague "Support for the Cuban People," the most popular option.

There are a few other hoops to jump through: You'll need a visa and proof of health insurance for the time you're on the island. Bring cash (U.S. credit cards won't work) and leave your tablet at home (internet service is sporadic at best). But if you're a seasoned traveler, especially one who speaks Spanish, arranging a visit to Cuba isn't that different from booking a trip to any Caribbean island. And if you're at all daunted, several travel agencies specialize in sending Americans to Cuba, and numerous organizations arrange group tours so you don't have to worry about the details.

Plan Your Trip

Location: About 100 miles (161 km) south of Miami in the Caribbean Sea/Atlantic Ocean

Getting There: Jose Martí International Airport in Havana receives nonstop flights from six North American cities (Fort Lauderdale, Houston, Miami, Newark, Tampa, and Toronto), and many other cities in the Caribbean, Europe, and South America.

When to Go: Cuba is tropical, with a wet season from May to September and a dry season from October to April. December and January are busy travel months; March and April have the best weather.

All trips to Cuba begin in Havana. This is the Cuba you've seen in all the photos, filled with classic American cars and domino players in cobblestone plazas. Highlights include the 18th-century Catedral de San Cristóbal and its surrounding central square, the 1929 Capitolio (modeled on the U.S. Capitol), and the Malecón, the 4-mile (7-km) waterfront boulevard linking Old

Havana with the more contemporary neighborhood of Vedado. Here is where you'll find Cubans being themselves: teenagers dancing and canoodling, fishermen catching their dinner, and old fogeys smoking stogeys. Depending on your perspective, Havana's two most famous nightspots are either tourist traps or must-dos: the open-air Tropicana nightclub, birthplace of the scantily clad Vegas showgirl; and La Bodeguita del Medio, Ernest Hemingway's favorite bar.

Cuba's gems aren't limited to the capital. Pinar del Rio, 100 miles (180 km) west of Havana, is the province where the nation's world-renowned cigar tobacco is grown and dried. You can tour a farm or explore the region's rich, red soil on foot, bicycle, or horseback. The colonial city of Trinidad is even more frozen in time than Havana. It thrived until the 1860s, when the sugar market collapsed, leaving its pretty pastel mansions and cobblestone streets behind as museum pieces. It's a great place to pick up a guayabera shirt.

Santiago, Cuba's second-largest city, is home to its largest Afro-Caribbean population. It bursts into song and dance every July during its Carnival celebration, when rumba music, conga drums, extravagant floats, Santeria ceremonies, and capricious costumes fill the streets. Baracoa, at the eastern end of Cuba, was first established by Diego Velázquez in 1511, but jungle-covered mountains largely isolated it from the rest of the island until a road was built in 1965. More than 50 years later, it's still free from mass tourism.

Belize

Swim the world's second-largest coral reef.

Central America's only English-speaking country covers just 8,867 square miles (22,966 sq. km)—it's smaller than New Hampshire, with a third of its population. But the small footprint is home to an astoundingly diverse geography, ranging from jungle to pine forests to savanna to coastal reefs and secluded beaches.

Scuba divers and snorkelers have always been drawn to Belize for the 190 miles (300 km) of coral reefs off its eastern shore. Belize's section constitutes about a third of the Mesoamerican Barrier Reef System, which extends from Cancun, Mexico, to Honduras, and is second only to Australia's Great Barrier Reef in size. A UNESCO World Heritage Site since 1996, the reefs support more than 100 different types of coral and attract over 500 species of tropical fish. In some parts of the country, the reefs are less than 1,000 feet (305 meters) offshore, making it possible to explore without getting on a boat.

Hol Chan Marine Reserve, at the southern tip of Ambergris Caye, is popular with divers and

Plan Your Trip

Location: Northeastern Central America

Getting There: A dozen North American cities have direct flights to Goldson International Airport in Belize City in winter, and more than half of those cities have year-round service. Ferries connect the mainland with popular island destinations like Caye Caulker (two hours from Belize City) or Ambergris Caye (about three hours). You can also catch a regional flight to the islands.

When to Go: Peak tourism season begins in November and ends in May, with the driest months coming in February, March, and April. The lack of rain makes for clearer waters for snorkeling and diving. Hotel rates are highest in December and January.

moray eels alike. It's also the location of Shark Ray Alley, where snorkelers (but not scuba divers) get up close and personal with southern stingrays and nurse sharks. Farther offshore is the famed

Great Blue Hole, a giant marine sinkhole 1,048 feet (318 meters) in diameter, ringed by Lighthouse Reef. A 2019 submarine expedition traveled 400 feet (122 meters) down to the bottom for the very first time, where it found a wall of stalactites, evidence that the hole was a dry land cave 10,000 years ago, when sea levels were much lower.

The attractions on land are equally impressive. Mayan ruins are strewn about the country, primary among them Xunantunich (shoo-nahn-too-nitch), as easy to get to as it is hard to pronounce. A hand-cranked cable ferry transports visitors (and their vehicles) across the Mopan River to the site, which dates back more than 3,000 years. Climbing to the top of El Castillo, the site's dominant structure, rewards visitors with spectacular 360-degree views of the surrounding valley. Lamanai Architectural Reserve, located in the north of Belize, is notable for the 90-minute riverboat ride that most visitors take through dense jungle to arrive from the town of Orange Walk. For birders especially, getting there is at least half the fun.

The flip side of Belize's diversity is its vulnerability. In 2018, UNESCO removed the Belize Barrier Reef from its list of World Heritage Sites in Danger, commending the nation for banning oil drilling, protecting mangrove forests, and restricting unsustainable development. But many natural threats remain. In addition to the hurricanes that impact the Caribbean every year, Belize contends with sea level rise, coastal erosion, coral bleaching, drought, and even tsunamis because of its location near the intersection of three tectonic plates.

Tikal National Park

Travel back in time to the cradle of the Mayan empire.

If you're only going to visit the ruins of one city from the ancient Mayan civilization, make it Tikal. Located in northern Guatemala near the borders with Mexico and Belize, Tikal sat at the center of the Mayan empire during its zenith between 200 and 900 CE. And some of its architecture dates back as far as 400 BCE. It's one of the best-understood Mayan sites, with a long list of dynastic rulers dating back to the first century CE.

Tikal is also enormous. At its height of influence, the city numbered up to 100,000 people, spread across an area of approximately 6 square miles (15.5 sq. km). The site includes more than 3,000 temples, plazas, terraces, and platforms, many of which must be reclaimed from the jungle periodically. It is estimated that only about a quarter of what once stood has been unearthed. Wide boulevards between sites, many of them shaded by tall trees, lend an even more expansive feeling. Tikal gets its share of tour buses, but nothing like the numbers of day-trippers from Cancún who visit Tulum or Chichén Itzá.

Tikal is one of the few Mayan ruins that allows visitors to climb on the structures. Star Wars fans

Plan Your Trip

Location: Guatemala

Getting There: Goldson International Airport in Belize City is closer to Tikal (about 4 hours by car) than La Aurora International in Guatemala City (10 hours or more drive from Tikal). From either of those airports, you can catch a connecting flight to Mundo Maya International Airport in the city of Flores, about an hour away from Tikal.

When to Go: High season starts right before Christmas and extends until spring break, usually in late March. The weather is cooler and drier then. Within this window, prices are usually more affordable in late January, February, and early March, except for holiday weekends.

love to ascend the steep steps of Temple IV (a.k.a. the Temple of the Two-Headed Snake), because it's the filming location where the Millennium Falcon left on its mission to destroy the Death Star. The 230-foot (70-meter) climb is vertiginous during the day, and maybe even more so in the pre-dawn

hours, which is.a popular time for visitors who want to watch the sun rise from the peak. You can also clamber up Temple II (a.k.a. Temple of the Masks) as well as the Central Acropolis in the Great Plaza. Another highlight of any Tikal itinerary is Temple I (a.k.a. Temple of the Grand Jaguar), where King Ah Cacao was entombed in 734. Climbing this pyramid, however, is prohibited.

No one is quite sure why the Mayans abandoned Tikal after so many centuries. The most common explanation blames overpopulation and overexploitation of the land's natural resources. More recent theories suspect extended drought made the area inhospitable, and a study in 2020 theorized that mercury and toxic algae poisoned the water supply.

Tikal's 1979 inscription on UNESCO's list of World Heritage Sites has largely insulated the ancient city from the kind of development and deforestation that has marked the surrounding region. Nevertheless, UNESCO still considers poaching, forest fires, and continued demand for land and other natural resources to be worrisome threats. Because Tikal is a major tourism attraction for Guatemala, ensuring its survival remains a top government priority. Your visit, when done in a sustainable manner, helps safeguard the site for future generations.

Monteverde Cloud Forest

Zip across the canopy in the birthplace of ecotourism.

When a group of 44 Quakers emigrated from Fairhope, Alabama, in 1951, they thought they were taking a stand against increasing militarization in the U.S.; Costa Rica, which had disbanded its army three years earlier, seemed just the right place. Little did they know they'd be birthing something called ecotourism. But in the 70-plus years since the pacifists purchased 3,460 acres (1,400 hectares) in the Tilarán mountain range, the land they named Monteverde—and Costa Rica in general—have become synonymous with environmental travel.

Costa Rica represents just 0.03% of the earth's surface but accounts for more than 5% of the world's biodiversity. The Monteverde Cloud Forest plays an outsized role in that equation. It is home to more than half of the country's 850 bird species (more than in the U.S. and Canada combined),

including the brilliantly plumaged quetzal. Nearly a third of Costa Rica's 1,500 species of wild orchids thrive in Monteverde's misty environs. So too do hundreds of species of butterflies. But because of the high elevation, there are few mosquitoes.

The 6 miles (10 km) of walking trails through the reserve are the easiest way to soak in the rain forest environment. (No specialty footwear is needed, except maybe in the rainiest season; regular walking shoes are fine.) Horseback rides are another popular mode of transportation through the jungle. But for a view that's literally above and beyond, try ziplining across the treetops. The Original Canopy Tour opened the world's first commercial zipline attraction in Monteverde in 1997, and it's still one of the best operations around. The ascent to the first platform is inside the shell of a tree that has

Plan Your Trip

Location: Costa Rica

Getting There: Monteverde is about a four-hour drive from either of Costa Rica's two international airports: San José, the capital, or Liberia, near the Pacific Coast. The route from San José is now paved all the way, but the roads between Liberia and Monteverde are a hodgepodge of dirt, gravel, and asphalt with potholes big enough to swallow a Smart car. If you're coming from Liberia, you might want to rent a car with high clearance and possibly four-wheel drive; try to arrive before dark.

When to Go: Monteverde has a wet season (June-November) and a slightly less wet season (December to May). Even when it doesn't rain as often, fog and mist still permeate the air. Rates are highest around the December and January holidays. Avoid Monteverde between August and November, when heavy rains make many of the trails (and some roads) impassable. May offers the best combination of good weather and low prices.

been hollowed out by a strangler fig. Gliding across steel cables from tree to tree is safe for anyone over the age of 5 and under 265 pounds (120 kg). For those daunted by dangling (but not by heights), hanging bridge tours offer similar vistas without the adrenaline rush.

Climate change is already modifying Monteverde. Almost half of the amphibians that once called the cloud forest home—including the golden toad, last seen in 1989—have disappeared. The temperature has risen by about 1°F (0.55°C) over the past 25 years, a difference barely noticeable to human visitors but critical to many of the native species. Combined with longer periods between rainfall, the higher temperatures have reduced the numbers of both quetzals and orchids, especially at lower elevations. Much of Monteverde's fauna has adapted to the environmental changes, following the cloud cover to ever-higher elevations. The flora, on the other hand, lacking legs or wings, has migrated much more slowly.

Panama Canal Cruises

Voyage between oceans in a single day.

Opened in 1914, the Panama Canal revolutionized shipping, saving 8,000 nautical miles (15,000 km) and multiple weeks on a voyage between the east and west coasts of the United States. But this 20th-century marvel of engineering continues to benefit cruise ship passengers over 100 years later by allowing them to witness the elaborate process that takes vessels from one ocean to another firsthand.

The word canal is a misnomer. Ships crossing from the Atlantic Ocean's Caribbean Sea to the Pacific Ocean pass through a series of locks that lift the vessels 85 feet (26 meters) to Gatun Lake, an artificial lake that delivers the 50 million gallons (189 million liters) of water needed to move each ship through the locks. At the western end of the lake, two more series of locks lower the boats back to sea level. The total distance traversed is just 50 miles (80 km) but the opening and closing of the locks makes the trip take all day.

Plan Your Trip

Location: Panama

Getting There: Trans-canal cruises leave from both coasts of North America. Los Angeles and Miami have the most departures.

When to Go: Panama's dry season starts in November and ends in April. That's the best time of year for standing on deck and watching your ship transit the canal without getting drenched. Few ships cross through the canal between June and October, which is hurricane season in the Caribbean.

For that reason, many travelers opt for voyages that only pass through one set of locks rather than a full transit. Many cruise lines offer passengers excursions like a tram ride into the Gamboa

Rainforest, passage on the historic Panama Canal Railway (the only option for crossing Panama before the canal was built), kayaking on Gatun Lake, or just going ashore to watch other ships go through the locks.

A wider set of locks opened in 2016 to accommodate ever-larger cargo ships and some of the massive 5,000-passenger cruise ships that have proliferated

in the 21st century (although the most gargantuan boats, like Royal Caribbean's *Oasis* class, are still too big to clear the Bridge of the Americas, which spans the Pacific entrance). But while the new locks are more efficient, the original 1914 locks are far more interesting. Barely wider than most of the ships that squeeze through them, the locks employ mechanical mules on either side to ensure the ships don't crash into the walls. If your ship doesn't cross through the old locks, you can always book a ride on a ferry that does.

Severe droughts over the past decade have lowered the water level at Lake Gatun, forcing some of the largest cargo ships to lighten their loads to cross through the locks. Conversely in 2010, torrential rains caused the lake to overflow, flooding the locks and forcing their closure. So far, the effects on cruise ships have been limited, but as the climate grows more chaotic, that may not be true forever.

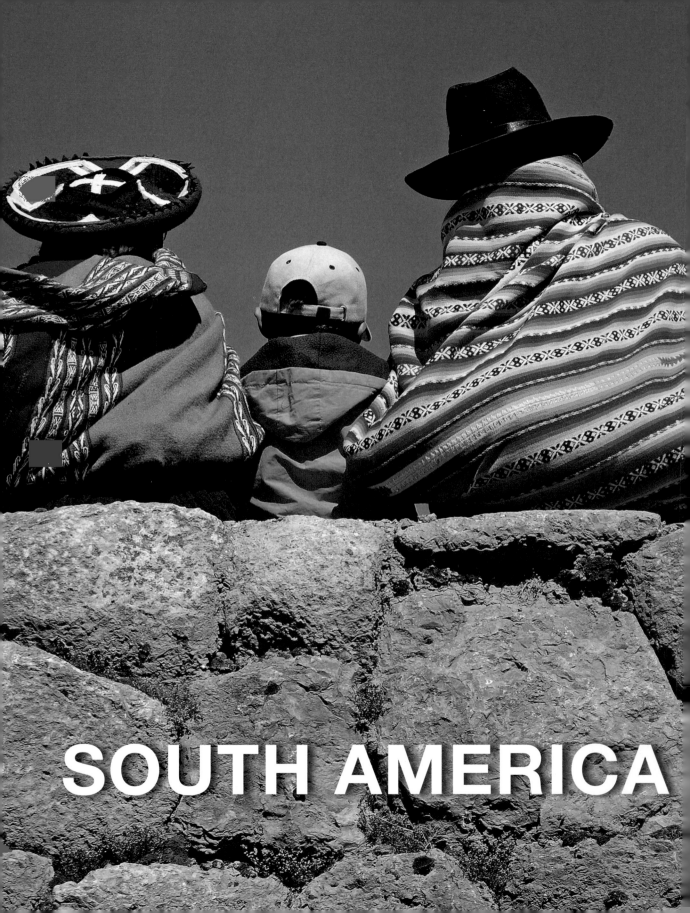

SOUTH AMERICA

The Amazon

The lungs of the planet let you choose your own adventure.

Spanning nearly 40% of South America, the Amazon reaches into nine countries and more than 3,000 indigenous territories. It is a river, a watershed, a jungle, and a rain forest, home to 10% of the world's biodiversity and a sponge for 100 billion metric tons of carbon.

The options for visiting this invaluable natural resource are just as multifarious. Half a dozen cities serve as gateways to the Amazon, each providing access to different facets of the rain forest. If you depart by boat from Manaus, Brazil, you'll be treated to a spectacle the moment you reach the big river: the "Meeting of the Waters," where the sandy Rio Solimões and the darker Rio Negro run parallel for nearly four miles (6 km) without mixing, before joining to form the mighty river.

Plan Your Trip

Location: South America

Getting There: Manaus, Brazil, receives direct flights from Panama City and half a dozen other cities in Brazil, including Rio de Janeiro, São Paulo, and Recife. To get to Iquitos or Puerto Maldonado, catch a connecting flight from Lima.

When to Go: You can't have a rain forest without rain. In general, it rains more often from January to June, a.k.a. the wet or high-water season. Rivers and streams swell, making it easier to explore by boat. In the low-water season (July-December), trails through the forest aren't so muddy. The dry season is significantly hotter than wet season. Bring mosquito repellent at all times of year.

While the Amazon is renowned for biodiversity, you're unlikely to see many large land animals, which usually stick to the deepest, most inaccessible parts of the rain forest. An exception is Brazil's Jau National Park, a UNESCO World Heritage Site since 2000 that is accessible only by boat. The park is home to more than 100 mammal species, including jaguars, giant otters, armadillos, and spider monkeys.

Iquitos is the capital of the Peruvian Amazon, built during the rubber boom at the end of the 19th century. From here you can board a multi-day river cruise to Pacaya-Samiria National Reserve or travel deeper into the jungle to a rain forest lodge—watch for pink river dolphins and manatees along the

river journey. Cruises usually offer a higher level of creature comforts, while lodges give a greater sense of being in nature. Many lodges lead nature walks through the rain forest—or above it on elevated walkways—to the best perches for birdwatching. Some even have their own boats to take you into secret swimming holes or to spots where you can cast a fishing line for piranhas (hopefully not one and the same).

Puerto Maldonado is Peru's other major rain forest gateway. It's less popular than Iquitos, perhaps because it's on the Rio Madre de Dios, a tributary, rather than on the Amazon River itself. But it's closer to Manu National Park (another UNESCO site preserved for its incredible biodiversity) and it's easier to combine with a visit to Cusco and Machu Picchu.

Tourism is low on the lists of threats to the Amazon, so you needn't fret too much about your visit contributing to its degradation. If anything, visitors who return from the Amazon better appreciate the urgency of preserving it. Slash-and-burn agriculture, logging, mining, wildfires, oil and gas exploration, and climate change are much greater threats to the "lungs of the planet." Already some 17% of the forest has been lost, pushing the Amazon close to a tipping point where it irrevocably becomes open savanna, largely devoid of trees.

The Pantanal

Search for jaguars, and the prey they search for.

The Amazon is an outstanding place to experience wilderness, but it isn't South America's best destination for seeing wildlife. Not for big land mammals, anyway; for that, you need to go to the Pantanal, the world's largest freshwater wetlands. Only about one-quarter of the size of the Amazon, the Pantanal is still massive. It's ten times the size of Florida's Everglades, or about as big as North Dakota. Most of the region is in Brazil, but small parts extend into Bolivia and Paraguay. And unlike the thick jungle of the Amazon, the Pantanal is a land of wide-open spaces.

The Pantanal is the best place in the world to spot the elusive jaguar, a spotted cat 50% bigger than a leopard and infinitely fiercer. The jaguar's powerful jaws are strong enough to crush crocodile skulls and turtle shells, putting them at the top of the South American food chain. Jaguars will eat almost anything, and in the Pantanal, they have an embarrassment of prey to choose from. The yacare caiman, one of the smallest members of the alligator family, is no match for a jaguar, unless perhaps all 10 million in the Pantanal could join forces. Jaguars are excellent climbers, so monkeys can't escape them in the trees. And they're strong swimmers, bad news for tortoises, iguanas, and even green anacondas, the world's largest snake, weighing in at up to

Plan Your Trip

Location: Central Brazil

Getting There: Cuiaba and Campo Grande are the best places to start your Pantanal adventure. Both cities require a connecting flight from Rio de Janeiro, São Paulo, Brasilia, or Salvador de Bahia (seasonal only). Cuiaba also receives flights from Belem, Belo Horizonte, Fortaleza, and Recife.

When to Go: Visit during the dry season (July-October) to maximize your chances of seeing wildlife. The Pantanal is gorgeous during wet season (January-May), but frequent rains may literally put a damper on wildlife safaris.

500 pounds (228 kg). Other jaguar prey abundant in the Pantanal include marsh deer, giant anteaters, giant river otters, and capybaras, the world's largest rodents (they're about the size of a fat golden retriever). Only the thick skin of the tapir, a sort of cross between a pig and a rhino, prevents it from being jaguar food.

Birds, on the other hand, have little to fear from jaguars. The hyacinth macaw, the world's largest flying parrot, is more at risk from poachers than from jaguars; they sell for thousands of dollars in

the illegal pet trade. Colorful toucans, parrots, parakeets, roseate spoonbills, green kingfishers, and scarlet flycatchers are among the 650 avian species identified by UNESCO, which designated 46,253 acres (18,718 hectares) of the Pantanal as a World Heritage Site in 2000.

Those preserved acres represent just a tiny 1.3% of the Pantanal. The rest is privately owned, mostly by cattle farmers, whose interests don't always align with those who seek to protect the Pantanal's undomesticated animals. Human activities like dredging, deforestation, and dam building are the most serious threats to the health of the Pantanal's jaguar population, not to mention the hundreds of other species it needs to survive.

Iguazú Falls

See 275 different cataracts and two countries in one visit.

Argentina and Brazil, South America's two largest countries (by population, land area, and GDP) have been frenemies for two centuries—in politics, trade, and, most heatedly, on the fútbol field. One thing the two countries do agree on, however, is the stunning splendor of the waterfall that lies on the border between them.

Or maybe that should be waterfalls, plural, as Iguazú Falls isn't just one cascade, but 275 different drops over a span of 1.7 miles (2.75 km). Both countries established national parks on their respective sides of the Iguazu River during the 1930s and have collaborated (mostly) to preserve the region and promote it as a tourism destination. Arguments over which country has the better vista are largely moot, since it's simple to visit both sides. North Americans don't need a visa to enter either country, and the border crossing is little more than a formality.

Brazil's Iguaçu National Park is about three times the size of Argentina's Iguazú National Park, but the Argentine side has more walking trails, ranging from a 1.5-mile (2.4-km) loop of the Upper Falls to the 10.2-mile (16-km) Yacaratia trail along the river, a route favored by birders. Each country also offers

Plan Your Trip

Location: On the Iguazú River where Brazil and Argentina meet

Getting There: Puerto Iguazú is about a 90-minute flight from Buenos Aires. Foz de Iguaçu is about two hours by plane from Rio de Janeiro or São Paulo.

When to Go: Unlike Victoria Falls, which dries up each summer, Iguazú wows year-round. South American summer (December-March) is the most popular time to visit, and thus the most expensive. March-May and August-October are less crowded.

a beeline trail to the Devil's Throat, a horseshoe-shaped section of the falls comprised of 14 different cataracts. To get even closer than the wooden boardwalks allow, take a boat ride to within misting distance of this colossal curtain of water. You'll definitely get wet, but you might not mind on a hot day. On the five nights closest to the full moon each month, moonlight combines with the mist of the falls to create nighttime rainbows.

Paraguay's Ciudad del Este is close to the falls, but not close enough for a view. It compensates with tax-free shopping, casinos, and hotel rooms that are usually less expensive than those in either of its neighbors.

UNESCO added Argentina's national park to its list of World Heritage Sites in 1984; Brazil's park was added two years later. Neither park is considered in danger, but the International Union for Conservation of Nature has expressed unease about shifts in water levels caused by Brazil's 2018 construction of the Baixo Iguaçu dam upstream. Hunting, invasive species, and agricultural runoff are also reasons for concern, as is a ballooning population that is outgrowing the existing infrastructure on both sides of the river. Limit your impact on this enchanting environment by recycling, walking, and using public transportation wherever possible.

Buenos Aires

Soak up old world charm south of the equator.

Argentina's capital city sells itself as the Paris of South America. And with good reason. Strolling down the city's wide, tree-lined boulevards past Belle Epoque buildings, stopping in at lovely sidewalk cafés, you can easily imagine you're in Europe. Buenos Aires pulses with old world charm, from its art museums to its public plazas to its grand bookstores to its *milongas*: dance halls where the tango is taught, practiced, and performed.

The 6,400 crypts, statues, and mausoleums at La Recoleta cemetery, built in 1822, recall Paris's Pere Lachaise necropolis, which opened 18 years earlier. Wander the narrow labyrinthine walkways between the sarcophagi in search of Eva Peron's grave, one of 90 Recoleta tombs that have been designated national historical monuments. Just beyond the graveyard sits the National Museum of Fine Arts, Argentina's answer to the Louvre or the Prado. Its collection includes works by Degas, Goya, Monet, Picasso, and Van Gogh.

The Teatro Colon rivals Milan's La Scala and London's Royal Opera house, both in its stunning architecture and its outstanding acoustics. The

Plan Your Trip

Location: Argentina

Getting There: Buenos Aires Ministro Pistariri International Airport receives direct flights from dozens of cities in South America and a handful of cities in North America and western Europe.

When to Go: Argentina's seasons are almost exactly opposite those in North America, so it's cool from June through August, and hot, sometimes exceedingly so, between December and February. Shoulder seasons are a good time to visit both in terms of prices and crowds; they too are reversed: March-May is autumnal, and September-December brings spring showers (October is the wettest month).

building originally debuted in 1908 and reopened in 2010 after a lengthy renovation. Another of Buenos Aires's magnificent old theaters, the Grand Splendid, was converted into a bookstore in 2000. The transformation restored Nazareno Orlandi's frescoes on the domed ceiling; the former stage is now a bar

and café where you can read any of the 120,000 books on the shelves.

But for its brilliant pink color, the Casa Rosada wouldn't be out of place in Rome or Prague. The Argentine house of government overlooks the Plaza de Mayo, a public square dating back to the city's founding in the 16th century. Every Thursday at 3:30 PM since 1977, the Mothers of the Plaza de Mayo have marched in front of the Casa Rosada in memory of relatives who were "disappeared" during Argentina's Dirty War (1976-83).

Buenos Aires has flooded multiple times in the past decade, presaging a future when rainstorms and heat waves both become more frequent and more intense. Population growth along the coast continues to cover up porous surfaces with buildings and roads, exacerbating the risk of flooding. The city has taken action to address these vulnerabilities, and these measures are also changing the look of the capital. In 2008, Argentina's Supreme Court ruled that no one can live within 115 feet (35 meters) of the heavily polluted Rio Matanza-Riachuelo on the south side of the city, and hundreds of families were relocated away from the river basin. The government has also installed hydrological sensors in the storm drains to monitor water levels across the city before they flood. A plan to plant 54,000 trees by 2023 aims to create a living sponge for both carbon dioxide and floodwaters.

Patagonia

Explore stunning icefields, melting at a faster-than-glacial rate.

There's something special about the ends of the Earth, and Patagonia may be the quintessential example. This 400,000-square-mile (1,035,995-sq.-km) region in southernmost Chile and Argentina is home to the third-largest glacial ice reserve in the world—only Greenland and Antarctica are bigger. The territory is replete with dramatic mountains rising steeply from grasslands, dozens of fjords, hundreds of glaciers, countless shimmering blue lakes dotted with icebergs, and a surprising amount of wildlife for a landscape that might initially appear barren.

The star of this show is Chile's Torres del Paine National Park, named for the three granite peaks that tower above the rest of the landscape. It's a mecca for hikers: trails with stunning scenery range from day hikes of just a few miles to the multi-day, 50-mile (80-km) W Trek (so named for the shape of the route). Regardless of how far you go, you're likely to see guanacos (cousins of the llama and alpaca) grazing on the grasslands at lower elevations, and if you're lucky, pumas (from a distance, of course). For glacier views without any hiking, drive to the south end of Lago Grey, where a boat will take you to the massive Grey Glacier at the opposite end of the lake.

Plan Your Trip

Location: Southernmost Chile and Argentina

Getting There: From Santiago, Chile, fly into Puerto Natales or Punta Arenas. From Buenos Aires, Argentina, fly to El Calafate, El Chalten, or Ushuaia.

When to Go: Any time other than winter (June-August) is a good time to visit. You'll have the best weather (and the highest prices) during South American summer (December-February). The shoulder seasons (March-May and September-November) offer a good mix of clement weather and smaller crowds. No matter when you go, expect fierce winds that might even knock you over. Visit during the new moon for dark skies and outstanding stargazing.

Chile's Carretera Austral is popular with motorists and cyclists alike. The 770-mile (1,240-km) route starts in Puerto Montt, in Chile's Lake district, and meanders past towering volcanoes, lush forests, and icy fjords before ending in the town of Villa O'Higgins. To complete the entire route, you'll have to take three ferry crossings. Farther south, near Punta Arenas, is Isla Magdalena, populated mostly

by more than 100,000 Magellanic penguins who migrate there to raise their young each summer.

Argentine Patagonia has a similarly breathtaking route between the towns of El Calafate, famed for its flamingos, and El Chaltén, 132 miles (213 km) to the north. The route is shaped like a sideways W, or maybe a backwards sigma S, as it traces the shores of two glacial lakes: Lago Argentino and Lago Viedma. El Chaltén is the gateway to the northern portion of Los Glaciares National Park, Argentina's largest park. El Calafate is a good base for exploring the park's southern half, which includes the Perito Moreno Glacier, one of the most accessible glaciers in the world.

Patagonia's glaciers are among the fastest-melting in the world. What was once a single icefield 18,000 years ago has been split into two separate regions. The Jorge Montt glacier, for example, retreated 8 miles (13 km) between 1984 and 2014. Climate change has played a large role in thawing Patagonia's glaciers, but it's not the only culprit. Plate tectonics are also pushing the land up, allowing hotter, more viscous mantle material to flow below the surface, hastening the melting.

Machu Picchu

Go now, before a new international airport brings
more crowds to these solemn ruins.

125

Peru's most popular attraction was built in the 15th century as a royal retreat for the Inca emperor Pachacútec. It lay hidden deep in the Peruvian jungle until 1911, when American explorer Hiram Bingham encountered it and announced to the world his "discovery" of one of the most intact pre-Columbian Inca settlements anywhere. Arranged along a series of agricultural terraces, Machu Picchu's nearly 200 surviving structures attest to the Incas' architectural ingenuity. Massive granite stones had to be quarried from bedrock and hauled up the hillside, then fitted together without mortar by master stonemasons.

Historians still aren't sure exactly why the lost city was built, or what purpose each of the structures served. There's evidence to suggest at least some buildings—the Intihuatana Pyramid, the Temple of the Sun, the Sacred Rock, and the Room of the Three Windows—were used to study the cosmos. The Altar of the Condor points to Machu Picchu's existence as a holy place. The aqueducts and architectural terraces, meanwhile, indicate a self-contained society that could feed itself. The high peak of Huayna Picchu affords panoramic views of the entire Urubamba Valley, fueling speculation that it was a lookout for enemy invaders.

Plan Your Trip

Location: Southern Peru

Getting There: The small airport in Cusco is the closest to Machu Picchu. It receives direct flights from Lima and Santiago, Chile. From Cusco you can hike the Inca Trail (usually 4-5 days) or take the train (3-4 hours) to Aguas Calientes. Cusco's elevation is significantly higher than Machu Picchu's (7,972 feet/2,430 meters), so many visitors head directly to Machu Picchu from the airport to avoid altitude sickness.

When to Go: April-June and September-November are the best times to visit. The biggest crowds are in the driest months of July and August. Heavy rains arrive in December (the month with the fewest visitors) and last through early March. Note that the Inca Trail closes for maintenance every February, the rainiest month of the year.

For many travelers, the Inca Trail between Cusco, where most travelers fly in, and Aguas Calientes, the town at the base of the hillside, is a bucket-list experience. You must hike with a local guide, and you can hire porters to carry your luggage. The 26-mile (43-km) trek usually takes four or five days,

but you can do it in one or two days if you start in Ollantaytambo, itself a worthy ancient site. The

hike is not especially difficult, but the altitude is challenging. It starts at 11,152 feet (3,399 meters) and ascends to 13,776 feet (4,200 meters) at its apex before dropping into the Urubamba Valley. Plan a day or two in Cusco to acclimate before starting your trek.

You don't have to hike the Inca Trail to get to Machu Picchu. The 3.5-hour train ride from Cusco to Aguas Calientes through the Urubamba Valley is one of the prettiest in South America. (In the rainy season between December and March, you may have to take a bus to Ollantaytambo and connect to the train from there.)

Machu Picchu was named a UNESCO World Heritage Site in 1983 and one of the New Seven Wonders of the World in 2007. In the past decade, UNESCO has repeatedly warned Peruvian officials about overdevelopment in the entire valley. Machu Picchu routinely receives more than 5,000 visitors per day, double the limit recommended by UNESCO. In 2019, Cusco's Superior Court ordered the demolition of a half-built seven-story hotel that was in violation of the city's cultural heritage ordinance. A new airport, scheduled to open in 2025, intends to bring direct flights from Buenos Aires and Miami, quadrupling the number of potential visitors to the already crowded region.

Chan Chan Archaeological Zone

Visit the ancient adobe city before it turns back into mud.

Peru's "other" ancient city was once the biggest in pre-Columbian America and the largest adobe city on the planet. Chan Chan was the capital of the Chimú society, an empire that once stretched from central Peru to modern-day Ecuador before it was conquered by the Incas in 1470. At the height of the Chimú empire, 60,000 people lived in Chan Chan, but it was largely abandoned by the time Pizarro's conquistadores arrived in 1532.

Like Machu Picchu, Chan Chan is evidence of an extremely advanced civilization. The 12.5-square-mile (20-sq.-km) site was divided by thick, high earthen walls into 10 autonomous rectangular "citadels" or "palaces," arranged in a social and political hierarchy. Today, more than 10,000 structures survive in a maze of streets and

Plan Your Trip

Location: Northwest Peru

Getting There: From Lima, take a connecting flight to Trujillo.

When to Go: April-September is the best time to visit. This part of Peru receives very little rain throughout the year, but summer (January-March) can be hot and muggy.

alleys, most of which are decorated with elaborate friezes, some of them hundreds of feet long. Even though the Chimú had no written language for recording measurements, the city's engineers were

able to build a 50-mile (80-km) canal to bring enough water from the Moche and Chicama Rivers to this desert landscape to sustain farmland on three sides of the city.

While water was a scarce resource during the Chimú empire, it now threatens to wash away the ancient city. Torrential El Niño rains that previously occurred every 30 years are now coming quadrennially, eroding the adobe walls and buildings faster than preservationists can restore them. UNESCO designated Chan Chan a World Heritage Site in 1986 and immediately listed it as in danger, where it remains. Peru's Institute of Culture has erected tents or canopies above many of Chan Chan's most vulnerable buildings and has used distilled water and cactus juice to harden the adobe of others. To protect them from further erosion, many of the friezes have been photographed and then covered with a reproduction so visitors can see what they looked like.

Severe flooding from the El Niño event of 2017 rendered much of the archaeological site off-limits to visitors, and there isn't much curation of the parts that are accessible. The Palacio Nik An is the only section that has been restored. To get a better understanding of the site, stop at the Chan Chan Museum before entering the ancient city, and hire a local guide to fill in the blanks.

Salar de Uyuni

Walk atop the world's largest salt flats.

It might be hard to picture the world's largest salt flats. At more than 3,900 square miles (10,000 sq. km), the Salar de Uyuni is approximately 100 times the size of Utah's Bonneville Salt Flats. That's all the more incredible when you realize that the entire flat, formed by the evaporation of Lake Minch some 40,000 years ago, sits at an elevation of nearly 12,000 feet (3,658 meters). Imagine if the top of Oregon's Mount Hood were the size of the state of Connecticut, and the immensity of the Salar starts to come into focus.

It is not hard, however, to *take* pictures here that deceive the naked eye. The Salar makes Florida seem hilly, with an average elevation that varies by less than three feet (1 meter). As a result, there's nothing in the background to provide perspective, enabling all kinds of trick photography. And during the rainy season (December-April), a thin layer of water

Plan Your Trip

Location: Bolivia

Getting There: The closest international airport is in La Paz, where you can catch a connecting flight or a 10-hour bus ride. Bolivia requires tourist visas ($160) for visiting U.S. citizens but not Canadians. All visitors to Bolivia must show proof of yellow fever vaccination.

When to Go: The flats have a high desert-like climate, with warm days, and nights where the temperature drops below freezing. The dry season lasts from May to November; June through August is the most popular (and most expensive) time to visit. The rainy season (December-April) is prime time for taking photos of the highly reflective surface, but be aware that heavy rains can cause tour cancellations.

sits atop the salt, turning the surface into the world's largest mirror. The Salar's otherworldly nature made it the perfect location to stand-in for the planet Crait in *Star Wars: The Last Jedi*.

The best way to cover this huge expanse is in an off-road vehicle. Typical tours of the Salar range from two to four days and include stops at the town of Colchani, home to a salt museum and salt factory; the Train Cemetery, where locomotives lie rusting away, abandoned after the collapse of silver mining in the 1940s; and the Laguna Colorado, a shallow, vermilion-tinted lake where two different species of flamingos flock in wet season. The Palacio de Sal and the Luna Salada, two hotels built almost entirely from blocks of salt, are popular lodgings.

One portion of the Salar that isn't pancake-flat is the Isla Incahuasi, located almost dead center in the salt deposits. The remnants of an ancient volcano, the "House of the Inca" is now a 60-acre (24-hectare) oasis of greenery, carpeted with giant 33-foot (10-meter) tall cacti seemingly dropped into the landscape from the Arizona desert. For about $2, you can hike to the top, where the views are practically endless.

Where there is salt, there is often lithium, and Salar de Uyuni is no exception. As much as 17% of the world's lithium lies beneath its surface. Lithium is prized for its use in electronics batteries. Perhaps the only reason that this pristine landscape hasn't already been plundered is that the lithium here is mixed with magnesium; extracting the lithium is costly, requires large amounts of water, and creates lots of waste. Still, in a country as poor as Bolivia, where GDP per capita is less than $4,000, it is probably only a matter of time before mining returns to this hauntingly beautiful place.

Galápagos

Tread lightly when you visit; invasive species—humans included—
imperil this unique environment.

Don't bother bringing your binoculars to the Galápagos. The animals you'll find here (and usually nowhere but here) are so unafraid of humans, they might just fog up the lenses. National Park regulations and rangers prohibit visitors from getting too chummy with the wildlife (i.e. within six feet/two meters), but nothing stops sea lions from hopping aboard the deck of your tour boat, or blue-footed boobies from dive-bombing your field of vision while you're snorkeling in the aquamarine waters.

UNESCO chose the Galápagos as one of its first 12 World Heritage Sites in 1978. The flora and fauna on these isolated islands in the Pacific are so unique that they inspired Charles Darwin to devise his theory of evolution during his 1839 voyage. They've been a living museum of natural selection

Plan Your Trip

Location: In the Pacific Ocean, 600 miles west of mainland Ecuador

Getting There: The only flights to the Galápagos depart from Guayaquil or Quito, both of which have international airports. A round-trip ticket from either of these cities is required, as is a $100 entrance fee, paid in cash (the U.S. dollar is Ecuador's official currency).

When to Go: The islands' proximity to the equator means they are warm year-round. But surprisingly, the rainy season (December-May) is preferred by many visitors for its calmer seas and better visibility for snorkeling and diving. North American summer (June-August) and the holiday season (December-January) bring the highest prices.

ever since. The diversity of species in the Galápagos is unparalleled anywhere on the globe, thanks in large part to the convergence of three major ocean currents within the 50,000-square-mile (130,000-sq. km) marine reserve surrounding the islands.

You don't need to have a Darwinian epiphany to be mesmerized by these islands. Simply walking among the world's largest and oldest tortoises—some weighing more than 500 pounds, many living more than 100 years—or swimming alongside the only penguins found north of the equator is enough to inspire a sense of awe. The islands themselves are also a thing of beauty, made even more wondrous by the lack of human habitation on most of them.

UNESCO added the Galápagos to its list of sites in danger in 2007 because of the threat posed by invasive species, unchecked tourism, and over-fishing, but reversed its decision three years later after Ecuador's government implemented strong conservation measures like charging a $100 entry fee, limiting the number of boats, and requiring a park ranger to accompany all trips.

Tourism has nearly doubled since 2007 to more than 270,000 visitors in 2019. But the revenue produced by all those arrivals has aided conservation efforts and helped to sustain the local population. Because of the

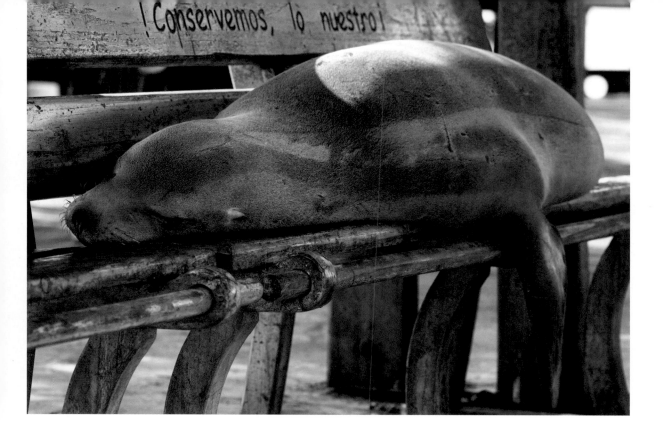

strict limitation on the number of boats, there has been an explosion in land-based tourism, in which visitors stay in hotels on one of the larger islands and take day trips to the more remote ones. The increase in tourism has brought with it a corresponding jump in the resident population required to serve all those visitors. Each additional person arriving in the Galápagos augments the risk of bringing invasive species to the islands. Illegal fishing and chaotic El Niño and La Niña weather patterns are also serious threats to the marine life.

Rapa Nui (Easter Island)

A visit to this extremely remote island dispels some myths, but not all of them.

By the time the first Europeans arrived on Easter Island in 1722, the civilization that carved and transported the 900+ massive stone statues known as *moai* had dwindled to fewer than 1,000 people. Exactly how, why, and when their ancestors built these oversized sculptures centuries earlier remains a mystery to historians and archaeologists. So too do the reasons for the island's deforestation. Once carpeted in the kind of lush palms you'd expect to find in Polynesia, Rapa Nui (the local name for both the island and its people) is now almost completely treeless.

A visit to Easter Island unearths the truth about some other Rapa Nui myths. For starters, while Chile is the closest country to Rapa Nui (the nation

Plan Your Trip

Location: In the South Pacific, more than 2,000 miles (3,218 km) west of mainland Chile

Getting There: LATAM is the only airline that flies to Easter Island; it offers departures several times a week from Santiago. Note that high winds often cause flight delays or cancellations.

When to Go: The dry season between October and February is the most popular time of year. The Tapati festival, held during the first two weeks of February, celebrates the Rapa Nui cultural heritage with athletic, artistic, and culinary competitions. April is the cruelest month in terms of rain.

annexed the island in 1888 but didn't grant citizenship to the Rapa Nui people until 1966), it isn't exactly close. Easter Island is more than 2,000 miles (3,218 km) from the mainland, accessible to visitors by a six-hour flight from Santiago.

For another, the *moai* have bodies. You probably haven't seen them because the most popular photos show them buried up to their necks in an overgrown quarry. But in other parts of the island, you'll glimpse them in their full stature, some as tall as 32 feet high (10 meters). The *moai* aren't located where they were originally erected, either. They were placed in their current positions by European explorers and archaeologists, who found the statues toppled when they arrived. Some historians believe the statues were felled during a civil war as the island's natural resources dwindled.

You also might not realize that the Rapa Nui people continue to inhabit the Isla de Pascua, as it's known in Spanish. The population shrunk to just over 100 residents in 1877, thanks to diseases introduced by European explorers and Peruvian slave raids. But the 2017 Chilean census counted more than 7,000 residents on the island, almost half of whom identified themselves as Rapa Nui.

Rapa Nui has been a UNESCO World Heritage Site since 1995. But that designation might not protect it from climate change. Because so many of the *moai* were placed right on the coast, they are extremely vulnerable to sea level rise. Larger, stronger waves pelting the shore will exacerbate erosion of the basalt platforms on which the statues sit. That could cause many of the *moai* to fall a second time. Reduced rainfall is also expected to bring drought. And in October 2022, a suspicious fire irreparably burned hundreds of *moai* near the Rano Raraku volcano.

EUROPE

Iceland

See geysers, glaciers, geothermal pools, and waterfalls in a country the size of Kentucky.

So many of Iceland's facets are matters of perspective. Most of the country sits just below the Arctic Circle, which makes for summers when the sun never fully sets, but also winters with almost no daylight. For some visitors, the extremes in daylight are reason not to visit between September and March. For others, those months present many more opportunities to see the Northern Lights—and many more hours to enjoy Reykjavik's legendary nightlife.

Iceland is largely treeless, thanks to the 9th-century Vikings who chopped down the coastal birch forests to clear land for planting and grazing and used the timber to build forges, homes, and saunas. But the lack of trees is also what gives Iceland's sweeping vistas their stark beauty. Meanwhile, efforts to help reforest the land often start by planting beautiful purple lupine flowers to stabilize the nutrient-poor soil.

One of the main reasons people visit Iceland is to see glaciers: 300 of them, covering 10% of the country's land mass. Every single glacier is melting, and some are retreating by more than 1,000 feet (305 meters) annually. But with the melting comes calving, creating more chances to witness truck-sized chunks of ice detach from a glacier and crash dramatically into the water below. As the glaciers melt, they uncover volcanoes, which become more likely to erupt—a boon for tourism but a blow to

Plan Your Trip

Location: North Atlantic Ocean

Getting There: Reykjavik's Keflavik Airport receives direct flights from most European capitals and a dozen North American cities.

When to Go: Icelandic summers are short, but the days are long from May–September. July and August have the warmest weather, but rain and heavy winds are not uncommon. May and September are less crowded than midsummer, but there's a chance some roads might not be open due to a late spring snow or early fall blizzard Sightings of orcas, dolphins and minke, humpback, and blue whales peak in June–July.

farmers because of the ash and lack of sunshine for their crops.

Tourism itself is also a two-edged sword. International visitor numbers skyrocketed from 300,000 in 2009 to more than two million in 2018. The influx helped save Iceland's economy after the banking collapse of 2008; but all those plane trips have led to the highest CO_2 emissions per capita in Europe, hastening the demise of the glaciers. If you visit, explore ways to offset your carbon, shop at local businesses, take the scenic route, and reduce your waste footprint.

The one thing visitors and Icelanders alike agree on is that the Blue Lagoon is a highlight. The lake-size spa is the result of a happy accident in 1976, when superheated water from a nearby geothermal power plant formed a large pool, attracting local residents, who started soaking in the 100°F (38°C) water. One of the earliest bathers found the lagoon's combination of minerals didn't just make the water appear blue, it alleviated his psoriasis symptoms. A cottage industry has since sprung up around the lagoon, catering to more than a million visitors, with changing facilities, in-water bars, spa facilities, three restaurants, and two hotels.

Dublin

Walking tours or pub crawls through Ireland's capital might soon involve swimming.

Ireland's Fair City jams a lot into a relatively small package. The Dublin metropolitan area's population is 1.3 million, about the same size as Louisville, Kentucky, but its appeals rival that of a major world capital. The greatest challenge for visitors is simply choosing *which* Dublin to experience.

First, there is historic Dublin. Christ Church Cathedral (Cathedral of the Holy Trinity) was originally erected in 1030 and is renowned for its gorgeous floor tiles and the 14th-century copy of the Magna Carta held in its crypt. The upstart St. Patrick's Cathedral, built on the location where Ireland's patron saint baptized people 1,500 years ago, was supposedly intended to replace Christ Church in 1191, but the two have managed to co-exist now for more than 800 years. Kilmainham Gaol, located just outside the city, is a former

Plan Your Trip

Location: Ireland, North Atlantic Ocean

Getting There: Dublin Airport receives flights from most European capitals and more than a dozen cities in North America.

When to Go: Expect rain at any time of year in Dublin. The capital is most crowded in summer (June-August). You'll find better deals on airfares and accommodations in the less popular months of May and September.

18th-century prison where leaders of the 1916 rebellion were incarcerated and later executed.

Then there is literary Dublin, designated a City of Literature by UNESCO in 2010. Since it

opened in 1732, Trinity College's magnificent Old Library has been the home of the Book of Kells, a 9th-century illuminated manuscript of the New Testament's four Gospels. Another 200,000 of the library's oldest and most treasured volumes line the walls of the Long Room, which *wasn't* the setting for the Hogwarts library but probably *was* the inspiration for the Jedi Archives in *Star Wars Episode II: Attack of the Clones*. Trinity alumni include literary luminaries Bram Stoker, Oscar Wilde, and Jonathan Swift. More contemporary authors like Anne Enright and Roddy Doyle are frequent guests at Dublin's numerous writers' festivals. In 2022, the capital celebrated the 100th anniversary of *Ulysses*, masterwork of its favorite son James Joyce; you'll get a great feel for Dublin just by taking a walking tour through Leopold Bloom's footsteps.

Finally, there is drinking Dublin. Even teetotalers can enjoy a visit to one of the city's 750 pubs, which are a center of social activity as much as they are a place to raise a glass. The city's oldest pub, the Brazen Head, was built in 1198; the Stag's Head, dating to around 1770, is a newcomer by comparison. To see where so many of those pints came from, stop in at the original Guinness Brewery in St. James's Gate, now a popular museum dedicated to the history of the world-famous stout. The top floor Gravity Bar is a great place to try your hand at the perfect pour or just to admire the view.

Recent reports by several climate organizations found that sea levels around Ireland were rising

twice as fast as previously predicted. That's bad news for Dublin, as well as other Irish coastal cities like Galway, Wexford, Limerick, Cork, and Belfast. A global temperature rise of just 2.7° F (1.5° C) would leave large parts of these cities underwater by 2040 and would bring the kind of heat waves that used to happen once a decade every three years. Ironically, both drought and episodes of heavy rain are predicted to become more common and more severe as temperatures rise.

Giant's Causeway

Walk through a legendary landscape.

According to legend, this striking landscape was built by the giant Finn McCool, who hurled some 40,000 black basalt columns into the Irish Sea to create a land bridge to Scotland. As folklore so often does, the story gets a little squishy from there. Some say he built the causeway so he could fight the Scottish giant Benandonner without getting his feet wet. Other versions claim McCool was a lover, not a fighter, and laid the stones so he could visit a Scottish lass he fancied.

The actual story of how the causeway came to be is no less colorful. Some 60 million years ago, as the North American landmass began to separate from Europe, volcanic activity created a large lake of lava on Ireland's northern coast. As the lava cooled, it fractured into the hexagonal columns we see today. In some sections, the columns form a level surface that almost looks like a cobblestoned plaza. In others, the columns vary in height, creating a series of multi-dimensional stair steps that some have compared to an oversized pipe organ.

Plan Your Trip

Location: County Antrim, Northern Ireland, United Kingdom

Getting There: The Causeway is about an hour's drive from Belfast International Airport or City of Derry (a.k.a. Londonderry) Airport. Dublin Airport, in the Republic of Ireland, is about three hours away.

When to Go: The Causeway is entirely outdoors, so it's best to visit between April and October, when the weather is warm and days are long. The columns may become slick when wet, so visiting in the rain is not advised.

The architectural award-winning visitor center is quarried from the same type of basalt as the causeway itself and is a good starting point for exploring the area. Several walks catering to visitors of varying ability levels leave from here or near here. The shortest and most popular is the easy 0.8-mile (1.2-km) Blue Trail, which ends at a rock that looks like a giant's boot. At the Portnaboe Bay viewpoint, keep an eye out for the formation known as Humphrey the camel. The 2-mile (3.2-km) Red Trail is a clifftop walk to the Shepherd's Steps, 162 very steep stairs down to sea. The wheelchair-accessible Green Trail leads to the town of Runkerry Beach through territory favored by skylarks and other birds.

The Causeway has been a visitor attraction for more than 300 years. UNESCO designated the 173-acre (70-hectare) campus Northern Ireland's first World Heritage Site in 1986, a move that has helped protect the region from overdevelopment. The National Trust, the United Kingdom's largest conservation charity, has managed the site since 2005. The greatest threat to the causeway is coastal erosion and rising sea level, either of which could severely alter (or even completely cut off) visitor access to the unique columns. Some scientific models even predict landslides that might bury the causeway under rubble that even a giant couldn't remove, neither for love nor valor.

London

There's so much to see before the flooding arrives.

Britain's capital has been one of the most popular destinations for Americans since the days when it demanded taxation without representation from its North American colonies. London is English-speaking and rich in history, art, theater, architecture, and of course the pomp and pageantry of the monarchy. These days, the food is even on par with the world-class attractions.

Buckingham Palace is the first stop on many London itineraries. Public rooms of the King's residence are open for tours from late July through early October. Visit at 11 AM to witness the Changing of the Guard. Monarchs of earlier eras made their home at the Tower of London. Built in the 11th century by William the Conqueror, it's the current home of the crown jewels and the site of centuries of bloody history. Henry VI was murdered here during the War of the Roses; Anne Boleyn was beheaded on Tower Green; Sir Walter Raleigh, Guy Fawkes, and even Elizabeth I (before she became queen) are among those who have been imprisoned in the Tower's dungeon.

Adjacent to the Tower is Tower Bridge, the iconic Thames crossing that many people mistakenly think of as London Bridge. Its glass-floored span is a spectacular place to look down on the river or up at the surrounding skyline. For an even higher vista, climb the 334 steps to Big Ben's newly refurbished belfry. Or ride the London Eye, where you'll ascend 443 feet (135 meters) at the wheel's apogee.

London's museums are without peer and often free. The massive British Museum's collection includes more than 8 million works, only 80,000 of which are on display at any time. They include some of the most famous artifacts in history, like the Rosetta Stone and the marble sculptures stolen taken from the Parthenon. Admission is free, but reserved tickets are recommended. The Tate Britain is home to the largest collection of J. M. W. Turner paintings, while its sister museum across the Thames, the Tate Modern, features works by artists ranging from Picasso to Jenny Holzer. Opened in 2000, the museum was transformed from the turbines, chimney, and oil tanks of a decommissioned power station.

Visitors to London are usually advised to bring a bumbershoot (umbrella). In future, they may want to add wellies (rubber boots). Climatologists expect torrential rains—like the ones that flooded tube stations in July 2021—will double in frequency by 2070. That's a serious problem, since most of the city's premier attractions are within flooding distance of the Thames. But areas beyond the floodplain will suffer too, especially in the low-lying East End and south of the river. As London expands its footprint and green space is converted to buildings and parking lots, there's no longer enough permeable land to absorb heavy rains.

Plan Your Trip

Location: England, United Kingdom

Getting There: Heathrow International is one of the largest airports in the world. Gatwick International receives shorter-haul flights from western Europe, and the occasional trans-Atlantic flight.

When to Go: Spring (March-May), especially after Easter, has the best combination of mild weather and low hotel prices. Summer (June-August) is high tourism season. Fall (September-November) is as temperate as spring and usually not as rainy. Store windows decorated for Christmas (and January sales) are two reasons you might want to visit in winter (December-February).

White Cliffs of Dover

The erstwhile bulwark against invaders now welcomes visitors.

Immortalized by Shakespeare in *King Lear*, the White Cliffs of Dover serve as a symbol of British pride. Looming high above the English Channel, they have played a critical role in England's national defense since 55 BCE, when they repelled an invasion by Julius Caesar. More recently, the 350-foot (107-meter) cliffs were a sight for sore eyes for British and French troops soldiers retreating across the Channel from Dunkirk. Later in World War II, a series of tunnels dug during the Napoleonic wars were converted into Winston Churchill's military headquarters.

The scene today is significantly more serene. Twenty years ago, the U.K.'s National Trust brought in semi-wild Exmoor ponies to keep unwanted brush at bay atop the cliffs, allowing orchids and other flowers to thrive in the grassland. Peregrine falcons and endangered skylarks soar high above, while butterflies (including the rare blue Adonis, a symbol of peace) float closer to earth. Local residents walk their dogs along the miles of public footpaths on the headlands. History buffs descend the 125 steep steps for the popular

Plan Your Trip

Location: Dover, England

Getting There: Dover is a two-hour drive or 90-minute train ride from London. From the Dover Priory train station, you can take a taxi to the cliffs or walk the 2-mile (3.2-km) footpath.

When to Go: Summer (July-August) is the warmest and most popular season. There are fewer visitors in shoulder seasons (April-May and September-October).

hard-hat and headlamp tour of the Fan Bay Deep Shelter tunnel complex, built in 1940-1941 to house a battery of artillery 75 feet (23 meters) below ground. Lighthouse fans walk all the way to the east end of the cliffs, where the Victorian-era South Foreland lighthouse alerts passing ships to a nearby sandbar nicknamed the Great Ship Swallower.

While the views from the headlands are phenomenal, they don't quite capture the imposing presence that has made the cliffs so impregnable. Perhaps the best way to appreciate that is the way previous would-be invaders did: from the deck of a ship. But if you don't want to go all the way to Calais, you can get a reasonable facsimile view from Dover Marina, St. Margaret's Bay, or Shakespeare Beach, popular with Channel swimmers because it is the closest point to France.

For future generations, the cliffs might be merely the stuff of history and literature. For the past seven millennia, the chalk that gives the cliffs their milky white color eroded at a rate of about 1-2 inches (2-5 cm) annually. But in the last 150 years, the rate had increased to 10 inches (25 cm) per year. Large hunks of cliff fell into the Channel in 2001, 2012, and 2021. What accounts for this literal sea-change? Scientists chalk it up to stronger and more frequent storms, and to the gradual disappearance of Dover's wide beaches, which previously shielded the cliffs from the corrosive effects of wind and rain.

Stonehenge

Get yourself to this ancient, enigmatic landmark before the rodents get to it.

Archaeologists have been able to pinpoint the era when Stonehenge was built (nearly 5,000 years ago), but historians still can't agree on how ancient civilizations managed to move 25-ton (22,680-kg) sandstone blocks from 19 miles (30 km) away, or how they brought the smaller dolerite bluestones from west Wales, 145 miles (233 km) away.

Nor does anyone know for sure exactly why the stone circle was built. One theory claims that Stonehenge was a prehistoric astronomical observatory, because the alignment of certain stones corresponds to celestial events like solstices, equinoxes, and eclipses. Another hypothesis alleges it's a beacon for ancestral worship, while a third suggests that only supernatural powers could have erected such an improbable structure. Additional fanciful explanations include a landing pod for alien spaceships, a giant fertility symbol, or the handiwork

Plan Your Trip

Location: Wiltshire, England, United Kingdom

Getting There: Stonehenge is about a two-hour drive west from London and only about 75 minutes from Heathrow International Airport or a three-hour drive south from Birmingham International Airport.

When to Go: Admission prices are higher on summer weekends and holidays; lower on weekdays from September to May. Prices reflect the relative number of people visiting on a given day. Some believe sunrise or sunset to be magical times to visit, but the biggest crowds arrive between 11 AM and 2 PM.

of the Arthurian wizard Merlin, who in this theory flew the stones from Ireland and employed giants to

erect them in their current formation.

Regardless of how or why Stonehenge came to be (or perhaps because of the uncertainty), the site inspires wonder among visitors. The standard ticket price (starting at £20/$25 as of 2022) grants you access to a perimeter outside the monument, but if you want to enter the literal inner circle, you'll have to spring for the £48 ($59)

Stone Circle Experience. These guided VIP tours start before the site opens or after it closes to the general public; tours are limited to 30 people and fill up quickly.

UNESCO added Stonehenge to its list of World Heritage Sites in 1986 but has threatened to remove it if the U.K. continues with plans to build a two-mile (3.3-km) tunnel near the landmark. Conservationists worry that the excavation of the tunnel could seriously destabilize the ground beneath the giant stones. That by itself might not cause them to topple, but rodents might hasten their collapse. A 2016 report by the United Nations and the Union for Concerned Scientists warned that if global temperatures continue to rise at current rates, England's population of burrowing moles, badgers, and rabbits will multiply, as will the number of holes they dig in the soil near Stonehenge.

The Stonehenge World Heritage Site includes several monuments in nearby Avebury, about 25 miles (40 km) north. The stone circle here is larger than the one at Stonehenge but less complete. Its origin story is no less puzzling, but it's less crowded, and admission is free.

155

Netherlands

See how this low-lying nation's ingenuity has kept rising seas at bay for centuries.

One might expect the Netherlands to be one of the nations most vulnerable to rising oceans. More than one-quarter of the country (including the cities of Amsterdam, Rotterdam, Utrecht, and the Hague) is below sea level. But it is precisely because of this precarious elevation that the Dutch are so much better prepared than other countries to tackle climate challenges: they haven't had any choice. For centuries, the Netherlands has kept its surrounding seas at bay with an ingenious network of dikes, dams, canals, seawalls, and levees. Whenever a city experiences unprecedented flooding—New York City, for example, after Hurricane Sandy in 2012—engineers usually consult the Dutch for expertise.

Holland's ubiquitous windmills, for example, are more than just a charming image on a bucolic postcard; they were used to drain swamps. Amsterdam's legendary canals aren't just a novel way for sightseeing boats to show off the city's historic core. They were built in medieval times to protect the city by letting water into specific channels while

keeping it out of others. In subsequent centuries, as Dutch influence overseas grew, merchants realized the canals were a great way to move their wares through the city and out for export.

Plan Your Trip

Location: Northern Europe

Getting There: Amsterdam's Schiphol airport is a major destination for most European and North American airlines. A smaller airport between Rotterdam and The Hague receives visitors primarily from London and Barcelona. Amsterdam's Centraal Station connects the Netherlands to the rest of Europe by rail.

When to Go: King's Day (April 27) is a national holiday typically marked by concerts and other festivities throughout the country. Because King's Day usually coincides with the end of Holland's long dreary winter, Dutch residents pour out of their homes to celebrate *Koningsdag* outdoors.

The Netherlands' embrace of bicycling is another planet saver. The low, flat elevation has long made it one of the best places in the world to get around on two wheels. More than 12,430 miles (20,000 km) of bike lanes crisscross major cities, enabling visitors to sightsee (or even travel from city to city) on two wheels. Even the country's stances on cannabis (not legal but decriminalized and tolerated in "coffee shops") and prostitution (legal between consenting adults) derive not from a desire to attract tourists but from pursuing solutions to problems like drug addiction and human trafficking.

Most Netherlands visitors arrive in Amsterdam, but there are plenty of attractions beyond the capital.

The port city of Rotterdam—about 90 minutes south of Amsterdam by car or train—is the place to go for modern architecture. The city was largely destroyed in World War II and rebuilt from the ground up in midcentury vernacular. The 2014 Markthal (Market Hall) is the unofficial center of Rotterdam, packing residential apartments and office space into a horseshoe-shaped building spanning a public market with more than 100 stalls. About halfway between the country's two largest cities is Keukenhof Gardens, where every April and May, 800 different varieties of tulips (totaling more than 7 million hand-planted bulbs) burst into a riot of hues.

Notre-Dame de Paris

Watch France's most famous cathedral rise from the ashes of a devastating fire.

One of France's oldest and most recognizable landmarks, the Gothic Notre-Dame Cathedral sits in the heart of Paris, on the Île de la Cité in the Seine River. Construction began in 1163 and took more than 100 years to complete. Its rib vaulted nave and ornate buttresses were major innovations at the time it was built. Over the intervening centuries, it was desecrated during the French Revolution, witnessed the coronations of England's Henry VI (in 1431) and Napoleon Bonaparte (in 1804), hosted the funerals of countless heads of state, and been immortalized in an 1831 Victor Hugo novel.

It has also seen numerous alterations, renovations, and restorations, including a major overhaul in the 19th century after *The Hunchback of Notre Dame* called attention to the cathedral's sad state of repair. Since that renovation, however, weather and pollution eroded the cathedral's stonework (including some of its distinctive gargoyles), and the wooden roof rafters were starting to disintegrate from age. The spire added by 19th-century architect Eugène Viollet-le-Duc was rotting from water seeping through its lead exterior. Fire was becoming an existential threat.

Plan Your Trip

Location: Paris, France

Getting There: Paris's two major international airports, Orly and Charles de Gaulle, both receive flights from cities all over the world. The City of Light is also home to six different train stations connecting the capital to cities across France and Europe.

When to Go: "April in Paris" is the title of a famous song for a reason: it's the best time to visit. The weather is warm but not hot, and the summer crush of tourists hasn't yet arrived. August is a popular month for tourists, but it can be unbearably muggy, causing many Parisians to flee the city for cooler climes. Paris Fashion Week (usually the end of September) is one of the most expensive times to visit.

Ironically, after France's Ministry of Culture embarked a multimillion-euro effort to protect the cathedral, fire did in fact break out in its

wood-framed attic on April 15, 2019. Firefighters battled the blaze for 15 hours and saved almost all of Notre-Dame's most treasured artworks, religious relics, stained-glass windows, organs, and bells from irreparable damage, but the spire and most of the roof were incinerated.

Three years later, renovation of the cathedral is in full swing, in hopes of reopening in time for the 2024 Paris Olympics. But preservation experts say it might take decades before the building is completely restored. Just finding enough mature oak trees to cut down for the cathedral's massive posts and beams is one challenge. Another is quarrying tons of limestone by hand to replace damaged sections around the vault and lateral walls. Other tasks requiring the skills of extremely specialized artisans include repairing stained glass panels damaged by heat and smoke, restoring the choir organ, and crafting an exact replica of Viollet-le-Duc's spire (the Ministry of Culture rejected a plan to replace the spire with an all-glass version). In some cases, there just aren't enough craftspeople to do this painstaking work, so more will have to be trained.

As of 2022, Notre-Dame's interior was still closed. But visitors may wander around the exterior and watch the progress of the renovation. It's a rare opportunity to look back into the past and see how this architectural gem was originally built, and to look ahead to how it will appear to future generations.

Bordeaux

Tour France's premier wine region before it becomes too hot for growing grapes.

Bordeaux has been synonymous with wine since Roman times and the drink of choice among Britons (who call it claret) since the 12th century, when the future Henry II married Eleanor of Aquitaine, bringing the region's thousands of vineyards under English control. Bordeaux wines have also been among the world's most expensive since 1855, when Napoleon III asked vintners to rank their varieties by quality and price. Bottles from producers like Liber Pater, Pétrus, and Château Lafite Rothschild now retail for thousands of dollars.

You don't have to be a Rothschild or an English monarch to enjoy Bordeaux wines. Less heralded vintners abound throughout the region, at prices to fit any budget. One of the best ways to find the one you like best is on a winery tour. Dozens of vineyards offer tours of their facilities and tasting rooms where you can sample their Cabernet Sauvignons, Merlots, Sémillons, and Sauvignon blancs (reserve in advance). If you make the city of Bordeaux your base, you can visit several wineries by train or bus without worrying about drinking

Plan Your Trip

Location: Southwest France

Getting There: High-speed trains from Paris reach Bordeaux in less than three hours. You can also fly into Bordeaux-Merignac Airport, but unless you depart from farther away than Paris, the flight will take longer than the train ride. Driving from Paris takes about six hours.

When to Go: Harvest season (late August to early October, depending on the type of grape) is the best time to visit. Summers are hot and crowded with tourists. Spring and fall have better weather, fewer crowds, and lower hotel prices. The rainy season usually begins in November.

and driving. Bordeaux is also a pioneer in bicycle tourism and has set aside a network of car-free bike routes, including a 16-mile (26-km) route to the castles of Libourne.

You'll also be well-situated for a visit to the Cité du Vin (City of Wine), a museum of all things

grape-related, housed in a building shaped like a decanter. The admission price includes a glass of wine at the Belvedere, an event space atop the decanter, crowned by a massive chandelier composed of thousands of clear glass bottles. The exterior views of the surrounding region from this height are equally memorable.

You don't even have to be an oenophile to enjoy a visit to Bordeaux. The city is home to more than 200 UNESCO-listed buildings and monuments,

primary among them the 1775 Place de la Bourse. Already one of Bordeaux's most recognizable sights, the Bourse got a boost in popularity in 2007 when the world's largest reflecting pool opened in front of it. The Miroir d'eau (Water Mirror) measures 37,100 square feet (3,450 square meters) and is the site of free concerts and Sunday night salsa parties. On hot summer days, visitors delight in walking through the inch of water that covers the pool's granite slab surface.

Climate change will surely increase the number of people seeking to cool off in the Miroir, but it also portends a more disturbing development. Higher temperatures are starting to produce grapes with too much sugar, which, when it ferments, creates higher alcohol content. Other formerly unusual weather patterns—such as hailstorms, flooding from heavy rains, and spring frost—have destroyed the entire harvest at some vineyards in recent years. France has attempted to stem the damage by allowing Bordeaux's notoriously traditionalist vintners to introduce several new varieties of grapes.

La Sagrada Família

See it now and later, when it may finally be finished.

Barcelona's longest-running show isn't a theatrical production, a soccer rivalry, or even a political throwdown. It's a basilica in the middle of the city that has been under construction since 1883. The church, formally Basílica i Temple Expiatori de la Sagrada Família, is the crowning achievement of Catalan architect Antoni Gaudí. Between the laying of the cornerstone and Gaudí's death in 1926, he started and finished more than a dozen other noteworthy projects, including Barcelona's Parque Güell and Casa Milà, a wavy apartment building commonly known as La Pedrera. Those two, along with the in-progress Sagrada Família and four other edifices, have been protected as a single UNESCO World Heritage Site saluting Gaudí's brilliance.

Plan Your Trip

Location: Barcelona, Spain

Getting There: Barcelona Airport receives nonstop flights from cities on five continents (all except Australia and Antarctica). High-speed trains whisk passengers from Madrid, Spain's capital, to Barcelona in less than three hours.

When to Go: Like most destinations in Europe, Barcelona is busiest (and hottest) during the summer months (June-August). Spring (March-May) is less busy except during the weeks leading up to Easter. September may be the best month, as it has fewer visitors and days still warm enough to swim in the Mediterranean.

Gaudí knew the church wouldn't be completed in his lifetime, so he drafted detailed drawings and crafted intricate models for future architects to follow. But when he was killed by a tram in 1926, it seemed dubious that his vision would ever come to fruition. Just one of the 18 towers (12 representing the apostles, four for the evangelists, one designated for the Virgin Mary, and the tallest one in the center reserved for Jesus Christ) in Gaudí's original design had been completed. Work stopped completely during the Spanish Civil War (1936-1939) and was severely hampered by a lack of funds from 1940-1990.

But starting around the turn of the millennium, the Sagrada Família's salvation came from an unlikely source: the millions of tourists who flood the streets of Barcelona each year, and who have been more than happy to pay admission to witness the progress of the unfinished basilica. The influx of funds has allowed the project's lead architects to proclaim the church will be largely completed by 2026, to coincide with the 100th anniversary of

Gaudí's death (he's buried in a crypt below the main floor, by the way).

But you don't have to wait until then to see the architectural genius of Gaudí's design; it's already on display in the parts of the basilica that are open to visitors. He took much of his inspiration from nature, especially the 36 interior columns of the nave, which branch off at the top to support the towers and the vaulted ceiling. When completed, the Sagrada Família will be the tallest church in the world, at 566 feet (173 meters), but still shorter than Montjuic, Barcelona's highest peak, because Gaudí believed no structure built by humans should be taller than a creation of God.

There's sure to be plenty of fanfare when the Sagrada Família is finally finished, and lines for tours will be even longer than they are today. But the basilica has been a work in progress for so long that it may be a little anticlimactic to see it as just another completed church. Kind of how if you reattached the arms on the Venus de Milo, she might be just another sculpture.

Venice

Get lost in its maze of canals before it's all lost to the sea.

Venice is arguably the place least like any other place in the world. There's a reason Amsterdam, Bruges, Copenhagen, Hamburg, Manchester, St. Petersburg, and Stockholm are all sometimes called "The Venice of the North," and not the other way around. Sure, those European cities all have canals, but none has the combination of art, architecture, food, and history that make the actual Venice inimitable.

In other cities, visitors equip themselves with maps and apps to find their way. But one of Venice's greatest charms is getting lost in its warren of labyrinthine streets and alleys. At first, the feeling of wandering through narrow, serpentine passageways is disorienting, maybe even scary. But after a few (or not so few) wrong turns, you realize that Venice isn't all that big, and it's hard to go too far wrong. Plus the number of serendipitous finds increases the longer you wander. Losing yourself isn't the thing to do when you have to catch a train, but it's an invaluable way to settle into the pace of life here.

Meander long enough, and you'll eventually arrive at every must-see attraction. Signs everywhere

Plan Your Trip

Location: Northeast Italy

Getting There: Frequent train service connects Europe to Venice's main railway station, Stazione di Venezia Santa Lucia, in Cannaregio. Venice Marco Polo Airport is located on the mainland, about a 10-minute drive from Santa Lucia. It receives flights from all over Europe, and seasonal service from a few cities in North America, Africa, and the Middle East.

When to Go: Fall (September-October) is the best time to visit without the summer crowds or the winter rains that flood the plazas. Venice's Carnival celebration (the two weeks before Lent) rivals those in Brazil and New Orleans; bring a costume and book accommodations far in advance.

point the way to Piazza San Marco, fronted by the basilica of the same name. The piazza seems purpose-built for café-sitting and people-watching. Next to the church is the Palazzo Ducale, the seat

of government and residence of the medieval leader known as the doge. Basilica tours are free, but it costs €20 (about $24 in 2022) to go inside the palace, well worth it to see Tintoretto's massive *Il Paradiso*, in the main hall. You'll also get to walk across the Bridge of Sighs, an enclosed limestone bridge connecting the palace to the New Prison (only in Venice could a dungeon built in 1600 be considered "new"). The bridge's name derives from condemned prisoners' expressions as they saw Venice for the last time.

No trip to Venice is complete without a ride on its waterways. If romance is in order, hop on a gondola, making sure to haggle over the price before you board. Or ride the ferries (*vaporetti*) to experience the chaotic stream of traffic on the Grand Canal, where gondolas, water taxis, ferries, and private vessels all somehow negotiate around each other.

Venice is slowly sinking, by about 9 inches (23 cm) over the last century. Combine that with rising oceans and Venice could become a nonfictional version of the Lost City of Atlantis by the end of this century. High-water events known as "acqua alta" in Italian have increased in frequency and severity since the 1970s, with the worst flooding occurring in the city's lowest point, Piazza San Marco. If sea levels continue to rise, elevated platforms and rubber boots won't be enough to keep visitors (not to mention priceless artworks and thousands of local businesses) dry.

Pompeii and Herculaneum

Wander through these ruins before neglect and mismanagement ruin them again.

The most famous volcanic explosion in history took place in 79 CE, when Mount Vesuvius erupted for the first time in centuries, burying the nearby city of Pompeii in a blizzard of ash and pumice and the town of Herculaneum in a fiery mudslide of molten rock. Residents had little chance to flee, and many died where they stood just moments after the cataclysm.

The event was well documented by Pliny the Younger, who witnessed the explosion from the town of Misenum, on the other side of the Gulf of Naples. But it wasn't until the 18th century that archaeological excavations revealed a remarkably intact snapshot of the ancient Roman city frozen in time. The falling ash preserved Pompeii's main forum, the Capitolium, the Basilica, numerous public baths, and an amphitheater. Dozens of individual homes still stand, with their furniture,

Plan Your Trip

Location: The Tyrrhenian coast of Central Italy, on the Gulf of Naples

Getting There: Pompeii is 30-40 minutes by car or train from Naples International Airport, which receives flights from cities throughout Europe and seasonal service from New York. Herculaneum is about halfway between Naples and Pompeii; the villas at Torre Annunziata are about halfway between Herculaneum and Pompeii.

When to Go: Summer (June-August) is by far the most popular time to visit both ruins. You'll find shorter lines and cheaper hotel rooms in winter (November-March), when the weather is unpredictable, but never terribly cold. The shoulder seasons (April-May and September-October) offer moderate temperatures and fewer crowds than in the height of summer. Admission to Pompeii is free for the first 15,000 visitors on the first Sunday of the month.

tools, kitchenware, and in some cases, their owners, immobilized inside.

The city of Pompeii extended for 164 acres (66 hectares), or about the size of the Mall in Washington, D.C., but only two-thirds of it has been uncovered to date. The excavated portion of Herculaneum is about one-third the size of Pompeii, but it is even better preserved than its more famous neighbor. In 1979, UNESCO designated both ruins as part of a single World Heritage Site that also includes two lavish villas in Torre Annunziata renowned for their well-preserved wall frescoes.

Heavy rains caused the collapse of a portion of Pompeii's House of the Gladiators in 2010 and brought down a section of an arch in the Temple of Venus and a wall in the necropolis of Porta Nocera in 2014. These incidents shined a light on years of mismanagement, corruption, and neglect at Pompeii. With financial help from the European Commission and the Italian government, the multiyear "Great Pompeii Project" shored up vulnerable walls and buildings, restored frescoes, built sidewalks to accommodate disabled visitors, and installed drainage systems to prevent flooding.

Surveillance cameras now watch over anyone who might try to loot ancient artifacts.

The restoration also unearthed more than 130,000 square feet (12,077 square meters) of the ancient city and a treasure trove of discoveries within the additional acreage. A note scrawled on one of the newly excavated buildings may even change the date scholars think Vesuvius erupted, from August 24 to October 24. The renewed attention to this archaeological gem should preserve it for the foreseeable future. But you never know when corruption, mismanagement, and neglect will once again rear their ugly heads.

As of 2022, admission was €16 ($17) at Pompeii and €13 ($14) at Herculaneum. Numerous outfitters, operating both online and in person, offer combination tickets and tours led by professional archaeologists that allow you to skip the line for a fee.

Acropolis and Parthenon

Ascend to the literal high point of a trip to Athens.

Throughout Greece, there are acropolises (Greek for "highest point"), and then there's The Acropolis in Athens. This is the famed hilltop citadel where in the fifth century BCE, Pericles orchestrated the construction of several tributes to the goddess Athena, including the Parthenon, the largest Doric temple of its era.

The Acropolis is the first stop on most itineraries of Greece. It's no longer the geographic zenith of Athens—that distinction belongs to Mount Lycabettus, which wasn't within the city limits 2,500 years ago. But the Parthenon and surrounding buildings still stand as an enduring symbol of ancient Greek culture. The Acropolis is one of the country's most popular attractions, drawing more than 1.5 million visitors per year in pre-COVID times.

The name Parthenon salutes Athena Parthenos, Greek for "virgin goddess." It's undoubtedly the star of the show at the Acropolis, visible like a city on a hill from all over Athens. But it's not the only attraction here. In fact, if you purchase a

Plan Your Trip

Location: Athens, Greece

Getting There: Athens International Airport receives flights from 50 countries. From the Acropolis Metro station, it's about a 10-minute walk uphill to the ruins. Wear good walking shoes.

When to Go: Spring (March-May) and fall (September-November) are the best times to visit. Summer (June-August) can be unbearably hot, crowded, or both. Admission is free the first Sunday of every month from November 1 to March 7, and on the last weekend of September.

combination ticket at one of the lesser-known ruins, you can skip the line to enter the Parthenon.

The monumental gate that now serves as an entrance actually predates the Parthenon. The Temple of Athena Nike succeeded previous temples on a location atop a bastion that guarded the

entrance to the Acropolis in Mycenaean times. The Erechtheion is notable for its Caryatids: large sculptures of female figures that serve as columns supporting its roof. The remains of two theaters lie just below the acme: the Theatre of Dionysius and the Odeon of Herodes Atticus. The valuable artifacts from this area are in the Acropolis Museum, located about 300 yards (274 meters) down the southern slope from the temple.

As you might expect of a 2,500-year-old site, the Acropolis has undergone frequent renovations and preservation efforts. The most recent, known as the Acropolis Restoration Project, began in 1975 and was renewed in 2010 with funding from the European Union. During a 2014 investigation after a large boulder broke free from the hillside, Greece's Central Archaeological Council found "instability over quite a wide area." Athens's notorious air pollution is discoloring some of the marble structures and eroding others, while torrential rains have caused flooding that threatens the stability of both the hillsides and the ruins atop them.

Olympia

Travel to the birthplace of the Olympics, before flames of a different kind consume it.

Every four years from 776 BCE to 393 CE, athletes from all over Greece traveled to the city of Olympia to compete against one another in the most important sporting event of the ancient world. Unlike the modern Games, the original Olympics took precedence over anything else that was going on. Political differences were shelved, and a three-month truce was called in any battles that happened to be going on. (Also unlike today's Olympics, chariot racing was an event!)

The ancient Olympics remained wildly popular for another 400 years after Rome conquered Greece, before the emperor Theodosius I outlawed pagan celebrations in 394 CE. And the site of the competitions declined after numerous enemy invasions, earthquakes, and floods. A UNESCO World Heritage Site since 1989, the archaeological

Plan Your Trip

Location: Peloponnese peninsula, southern Greece

Getting There: The nearest major airport is Athens International, which receives flights from 50 countries worldwide. From Athens, Olympia is about a 3.5-hour drive or bus ride.

When to Go: The ancient Olympics took place in the summer, but there's no reason you have to visit during the hottest, most crowded time of the year. Spring (March-May) and fall (September-November) are much better choices.

sites of Olympia have been restored enough to let visitors imagine they can hear the roar of the crowd. You can even set your toes on the same stone

starting line where the ancient Greeks raced against one another—naked—for the glory of an olive wreath.

Olympia's other marquee attraction is the Temple of Zeus, which once housed Phidias's gold-and-ivory Statue of Zeus. One of the Seven Wonders of the Ancient World, the statue was destroyed in the fifth century CE, but the temple still stands as a tribute to the father of the Greek gods. Phidias's workshop has also been excavated; the Temple of Hera is where the Olympic flame is first lit at the beginning of each Olympiad. The nearby Olympia Archaeological Museum preserves artifacts found on the ancient site, while the Museum of the History of the Olympic Games of Antiquity features more than 400 exhibits, including an interactive theater.

In the 21st century, Olympia has witnessed a recurring event of a more troublesome kind: wildfires. Over a two-month-long period in 2007, a record heat wave combined with strong winds burned an area of 670,000 acres (270,000 hectares) across the south of Greece. The flames burned some areas of the archaeological site but spared the Stadium, the Temple of Zeus, and the statue of Hermes of Praxiteles. Another blaze in 2017 did less damage, as firefighters raced to stop the flames before they reached Olympia. And in 2021, high winds and record high temperatures (as much as 116°F/47°C in Athens) fueled another conflagration that forced residents in some parts of Olympia to evacuate. If global temperatures continue to rise, Greece can only hope these kinds of infernos don't become quadrennial events as well.

Dubrovnik

Stroll through the walled Old City before climate change washes away its appeals.

The thick walls surrounding the Old City of Dubrovnik are lasting evidence of how many different civilizations have tried to annex the "Pearl of the Adriatic" since its founding by Greek refugees 1,300 years ago. Dubrovnik has been targeted by everyone from the Normans to the Venetians to Napoleon to the Yugoslav People's Army in 1991.

These days, however, anyone can claim Dubrovnik as their own, even without bringing an invading army. The Old City has been a UNESCO World Heritage Site since 1979, the same year Dubrovnik was demilitarized in hopes of promoting tourism. UNESCO also helped restore the city after an 8-month siege by Serbian forces during the breakup of Yugoslavia in 1991. Dubrovnik's distinctive architecture may be familiar to fans of the HBO series *Game of Thrones*, which used the medieval city as the location for the fictional King's Landing, or to the millions who saw *Star Wars: The Last Jedi*, where it stood in for Canto Bight, a casino city.

> ## Plan Your Trip
>
> **Location:** Southern Croatia
>
> **Getting There:** Dubrovnik Airport receives flights from all over Europe, and seasonal service from New York.
>
> **When to Go:** Spring (March-May) and fall (September-November) offer the best combination of mild weather and lower prices and crowds. Summers are warm but not hot and usually dry, while winter temperatures rarely go below 55°F (13°C).

The Old City's main drag, Stradun (also called Placa), is completely closed to cars, making it an ideal boulevard for strolling and people-watching. The best café-sitting, however, is on the outside of the old city walls, in two outdoor taverns called Buza (Croatian for "hole in the wall") bars, carved out of the cliffs overlooking the Adriatic. From this perch, you can pick out your favorite beach, identify

the best spot for sea kayaking, or map out a tour of the islands off the Dalmatian coast. One of the more popular destinations is Lokrum Island, said to be cursed by Benedictine monks who were expelled from the island by Napoleon. For a bird's-eye view of the city, ride the bright orange passenger gondola to the top of Mount Srd. This is an especially popular sunset destination.

The impregnable walls of the old city kept Dubrovnik safe from hostile armies throughout the Middle Ages. But they may not be able to protect the old town against climate change. A 2018 Nature Communications study of Mediterranean World Heritage Sites found that Dubrovnik (and five other locations in Croatia) could be devastated by a 100-year storm surge, something that is now happening much more often than once a century. The news was sobering enough to Croatian and European officials that they developed a climate change adaptation plan for Dubrovnik that mitigates urban heat island effects of global warming. Measures include adding green roofs, planting trees and other shade structures, and converting paved parking lots to permeable materials. Hopefully, it will be enough to combat the rising tides.

The Alps

Climb every mountain before they melt like Toblerone bars on a hot day.

Europe's highest mountain range spans eight countries in a sweeping arc from France to Slovenia. These snowy slopes have hosted the Winter Olympics 10 times and are slated for an 11th in 2026. The storied summits include Mont Blanc (the highest in the Alps) and the forbidding Matterhorn, whose nearly symmetrical peak inspired the shape of Toblerone chocolate bars, and whose steep faces birthed the modern mountaineering movement in the 19th century. Long before Mount Everest was on anyone's radar, the Matterhorn was the holy grail for climbers.

In the 21st century, neither crampons nor ice axes are required to enjoy the Alps' majestic beauty. Roads now lead to some of the most charming villages in all of Europe, and chairlifts and gondolas carry visitors even higher to lofty vistas of glaciers and alpine lakes and meadows. These days, the hardest part about a trip to the Alps is choosing which adorable town to visit.

Almost all vehicles in Zermatt, Switzerland, are electric, keeping the air as pristine as it was in 1865, when climbers first summited the nearby Matterhorn. In Lucerne, the eponymous lake takes center stage, but the town's most photographed landmark is the reconstructed Kapellbrücke, a covered wooden footbridge spanning the Reuss River. Montreux is familiar to fans of Deep Purple's

"Smoke on the Water," which references the 1971 fire that destroyed a casino. The Montreux Jazz Festival brings some of the most famous names in popular music to the shores of Lake Geneva every summer.

Innsbruck, Austria, hosted the Winter Olympics in 1964 and again in 1976, but made headlines more recently in 2007 with the opening of Zaha Hadid's Hungerburgbahn funicular railway stations. Chamonix is the gateway town for Mont Blanc and home to some of Europe's best skiing in winter and unrivaled hiking in summer. The 110-mile (170-km) Tour du Mont Blanc trail circles the Mont

Plan Your Trip

Location: France, Switzerland, Monaco, Italy, Liechtenstein, Austria, Germany, and Slovenia

Getting There: Most destinations in the Alps are easily reached by car or train from major airports in each of the eight countries crossed by the mountain range.

When to Go: Winter (December-March) for world-class skiing; summer (June-August) for swimming and boating on moraine lakes; spring (April-May) and fall (September-October) for hiking and fewer crowds.

Blanc massif, passing through France, Switzerland, and Italy. Aosta, on the Italian side of Mont Blanc—and reached via a 7-mile (11-km) tunnel underneath the mountain—dates to Roman times; its town walls, theatre, and Arch of Augustus remain largely intact.

Sadly, climate change researchers fear that up to 92% of the Alps' 4,000 glaciers could be lost by the end of this century. Already, ice caves tall enough for a person to stand in are hollowing out several Austrian glaciers from the inside. Meanwhile, as treeline inches up the slopes, a layer of white snow that previously reflected sunlight is giving way to sunlight-absorbing vegetation, accelerating the melting process. The loss of glacial ice isn't just an environmental tragedy; it's making the mountains more dangerous, especially for climbers, as avalanches and falling rocks now afflict slopes previously held fast by thousands of years of ice.

Vienna

Experience its medieval, baroque, and 19th-century charms before skyscrapers intrude.

The longtime capital of the Habsburg empire has been a Mecca of European music, art, and culture for centuries. Mozart, Beethoven, Schubert, and Strauss all called the city home at one time, as did the painter Gustav Klimt. Vienna grew up around Celtic and Roman settlements along the Danube River, with the ornate St. Stephen's Cathedral at its heart. But it was during the reign (1848-1916) of Emperor Franz Joseph that the jewel box city developed most of the trademark architecture in its historic core.

Franz Joseph incorporated 34 suburbs into the city and tore down the fortifications that previously served as the city limits, replacing those ramparts with a Ringstrasse (ring road) lined with stately buildings. Mozart's *Don Giovanni* was the premier performance at the Vienna State Opera in 1869; trading at the Stock Exchange started in 1877. The Greek-style Parliament and the Neo-Gothic City Hall both opened their doors in 1883, followed by the university in 1884. Gustav

Plan Your Trip

Location: Northeastern Austria

Getting There: Vienna International Airport receives flights from all over Europe and from major cities in North America, South America, Asia, and the Middle East.

When to Go: Vienna is at its best in spring (March-May) and fall (September-November). Like most European capitals, the city is at its most crowded during summer (June-August). The Music Film Festival (July-August) is a popular summertime attraction.

Klimt painted the ceiling above the staircase at the National Theater; the Kunsthistorisches Museum showcases the world's largest Breughel collection and other treasures from the Habsburg era. Dozens of galleries await just west of the Ringstrasse in the MuseumsQuartier.

A dedicated tram completes the 4-mile (6-km) circuit in about 25 minutes, but if you walk the route, you'll be able to stop and go into the buildings or sample a Linzer torte in one of dozens of cute cafés. A dedicated bike path around the loop makes the ring ideal for exploring on two wheels. At this pace, you'll be more likely to spot locations where remnants of the original walls still stand.

UNESCO inscribed Vienna's historic center on its list of World Heritage Sites in 2001 and added it to its list in danger in 2017, when a developer tried to build a 246-foot (75-meter) hotel, convention center, and indoor skating rink on the site of the old hay market in the historic center. Even after the building was scaled down to 216 feet (66 meters), UNESCO still worried that it would open the door to more high rises throughout the historic center, and ultimately ruin the appeal of the former emperor's ensemble. At its 2021 meeting, UNESCO retained the historic center as a site in danger because the Vienna government's development plans didn't bar future tall buildings from the protected zone.

The Berlin Wall

Witness a piece of recent history before too much of it goes the way of the Soviet Union.

The Berlin Wall has been gone for longer than it stood as the most tangible evidence of the half-century-long Cold War. Built in 1961 to stem the flow of millions of East Germans fleeing the Communist system into West Berlin, the barrier came tumbling down in 1989, abetted by the blows of ordinary citizens.

In the zeal to demolish this symbol of a divided Germany, however, only a few sections of the wall were left standing for posterity. The 100-mile

(160-km) Berlin Wall Trail is a pedestrian and cycling path that traces the fortifications that previously surrounded West Berlin. And in several sections of the city, a double line of cobblestones in the street mark the Wall's former location. But there are long stretches where buildings have been erected over the stones. In other areas, nature has reclaimed the land where the wall once stood.

The best place to start a Wall tour is the Brandenburg Gate. Built in 1788-91, it was inaccessible to Germans on both sides of the Wall during the Cold War. But it has been the symbol of a reunified Berlin ever since it officially reopened on December 22, 1989. Nine days later, Germans on both sides of the divide flocked here to celebrate their first New Year's Eve together in 29 years.

From Brandenburg Gate, walk 10 minutes to Potsdamer Platz, one of Europe's busiest squares before the Wall bisected it, and humming with activity again now that the divider is gone. An excellent exhibition here features heavily graffitied segments of the original wall (many with chunks chipped away by rogue souvenir seekers) interspersed with contextual displays. The exhibition was supposed to be temporary but was made permanent due to positive public response. On nearby Erna-Berger-Strasse, you can climb the last remaining East German watchtower.

About a mile (1.6 km) east of Potsdamer Platz lies Checkpoint Charlie, scene of many a spy movie and countless escape attempts by East Berliners. Historian Rainer Hildebrandt's Wall Museum here has been chronicling those and other escapades since it opened in 1963. On Bernauer Strasse, on the north side of the city, a picket line of unconnected poles stand where the Wall previously stood.

The longest extant section of the wall is the 0.8-mile (1.3-km) East Side Gallery, on the east bank of the River Spree. As soon as Communism fell, 118 artists from 21 countries began painting murals on the east side of this section of wall. It's now the world's largest outdoor art gallery, protected as a memorial since 1991. Some of the most recognizable images include Brigit Kinder's Trabant crashing through the wall and Dmitri Vrubel's depiction of a kiss between former Soviet premier Leonid Brezhnev and former East German leader Erich Honecker. For an even deeper dive into Cold War history, be sure to download the interactive Berlin Wall app from Chronik der Mauer; search "The Berlin Wall" at your device's app store.

Plan Your Trip

Location: Central Germany

Getting There: Because it was divided for so long, Berlin isn't as well connected to North America by air as Frankfurt or Munich. Both of those hubs have more nonstops from the U.S. and Canada than Berlin's Brandenburg Airport, which opened in 2020. High-speed Inter-City Express (ICE) trains connect Berlin to Frankfurt, Munich, and many other cities across Europe.

When to Go: May-September are the best, albeit the most crowded, times of year. If you don't mind icy, gray days, visit in November and December, when Berlin's Christmas markets are in full swing, and when you can partake in celebrations commemorating the first New Year's Eve after reunification.

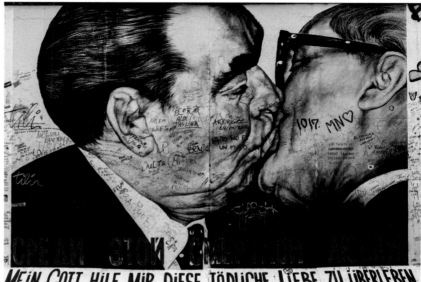

MEIN GOTT, HILF MIR, DIESE TÖDLICHE LIEBE ZU ÜBERLEBEN

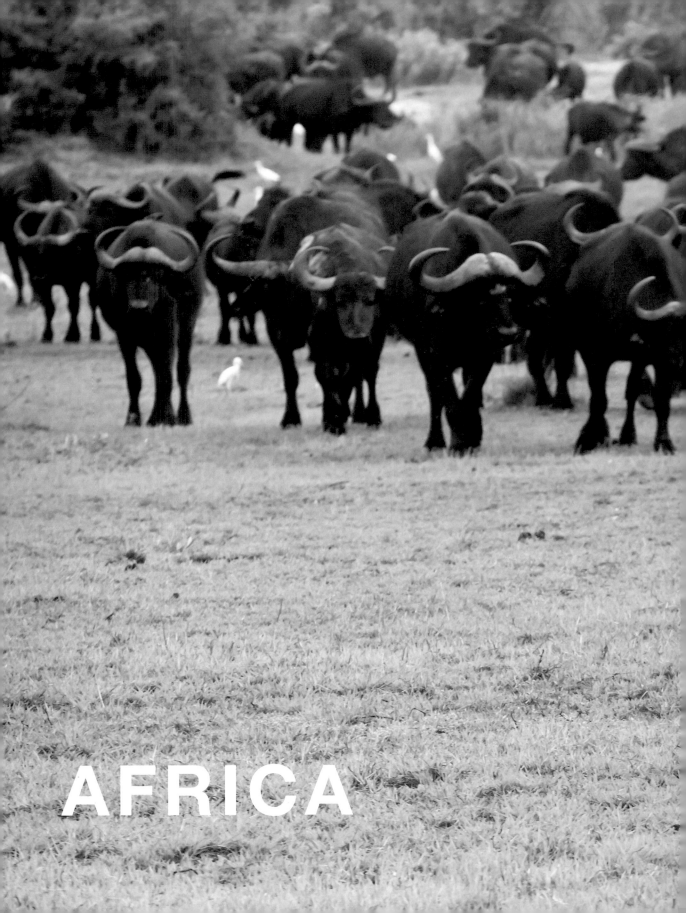

AFRICA

Kilimanjaro

Summit the "Roof of Africa"—or just wander its attic.

With a snow-capped peak made infamous in the title of a 1936 Hemingway short story, Kilimanjaro is Africa's tallest mountain, a dormant volcano topping out at 19,341 feet (5,895 meters), looming high over the Tanzanian horizon and visible from as far away as Kenya. It has been a UNESCO World Heritage site since 1987.

Because Kilimanjaro doesn't require any technical climbing skills, approximately 50,000 people attempt to walk to the summit every year, and about two-thirds of them make it there—and back, because as any experienced mountaineer will tell you, the peak is only the halfway point of any climb. This is not to say that the hike is a Sunday stroll. To properly acclimatize to the lower oxygen levels at higher elevations, most ascents take five to nine days, and all require the leadership of a licensed guide.

But you don't have to go all the way to the summit to experience Kilimanjaro. The national park is 661 square miles (1,712 sq. km) in area and includes plenty of sublime scenery at elevations that don't require supplemental oxygen. Numerous outfitters offer day hikes or mountain bike rides through the montane forest zone, a land of sacred cultural sites, crater-filled lakes, and secluded waterfalls.

Plan Your Trip

Location: Tanzania

Getting There: Several European and African airlines have direct flights to Kilimanjaro International Airport. You can also take a connecting flight from Dar Es Salaam, Tanzania's capital, or from Nairobi, Kenya, both of which are less than 90 minutes away by plane.

When to Go: Kilimanjaro has two dry seasons: from late June to September and from December to early March. The amount of daylight does not vary much from one season to another.

Wildlife viewing isn't necessarily the focal point of such an excursion, but while you're here, you might encounter some of Kilimanjaro's 179 species of birds or 140 mammal species, including some found nowhere else on earth. Colobus monkeys are some of the most common sightings. On the Rongai route to the summit, you might even glimpse an elephant or giraffe wandering over from Amboseli National Park just across the border in Kenya.

In 2006, the film *An Inconvenient Truth* predicted that the snows of Kilimanjaro would completely disappear by 2020 because of global

warming. As of 2022, that hadn't happened, but the mountain's iconic ice fields have retreated by 90% in the past century, and if trends continue at the same rate, the peak will be devoid of snow by 2040. Glaciologists say that's a function of naturally changing patterns of precipitation, rather than a consequence of man-made climate change. But regardless of the cause, the result is undeniable: a Kilimanjaro whose snows may someday appear only in fiction.

Zanzibar

Sample a little of everything Africa has to offer.

No matter what you're looking for in an Africa vacation, you're likely to find it in Zanzibar, the semiautonomous archipelago state off the coast of mainland Tanzania. White sand beaches overlooking warm, clear-blue Indian Ocean waters? Check. Reefs abundant with marine life for snorkeling and diving? Yep. Deserted islands where you can get away from it all? You betcha. Surrounding Zanzibar's two main populated islands are more than 50 atolls and keys, many of them uninhabited, where you can disappear for as long as you like.

A history steeped in influences from Arabic, Indian, Persian, and European cultures? They're all found in the architecture and urban fabric of Stone Town's old quarter, a UNESCO World Heritage Site since 2000. You could spend an entire afternoon just wandering narrow alleys in search of Zanzibar doors, stately double-wide entrances hand-carved from sturdy teak or ebony and lovingly decorated with brass studs, rosettes, or friezes.

Colorful markets and fresh seafood? Absolutely. Zanzibar is known as the Spice Islands because so

Plan Your Trip

Location: Zanzibar is an archipelago of more than 50 islands off the coast of Africa, east of mainland Tanzania. Most of its population lives on Unjuga Island (often referred to as Zanzibar Island) and Pemba Island.

Getting There: Several countries in Europe and the Middle East offer direct flights to Kisauni, the international airport on Zanzibar Island. You can also fly to Dar es Salaam, on the mainland, and take an inexpensive connection flight to Zanzibar.

When to Go: Zanzibar is near the equator, with a tropical climate year-round. June to September is the coolest period, still warm, with little rain. Mid-December to February is also dry, but hotter. July and August are the best months for scuba diving.

many aromatic spices grow and were historically traded here. If you'd like to do more than smell the scents of cloves, turmeric, cinnamon, nutmeg, and black pepper, you can tour the plantations and

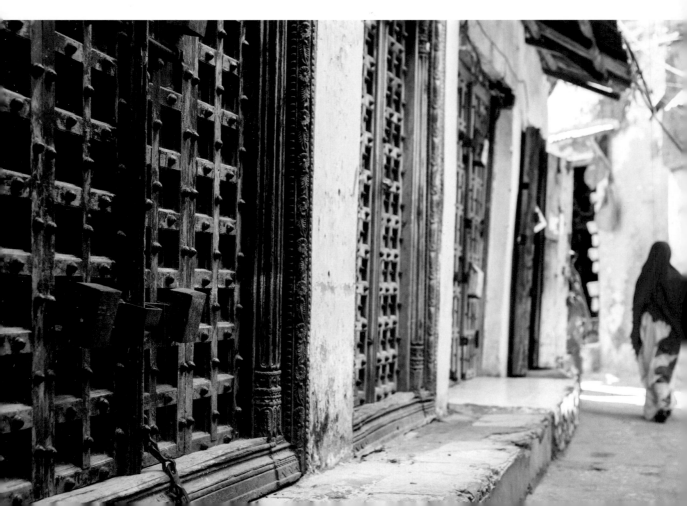

learn about their medicinal and culinary histories. Or just sample the food in the restaurants and street markets.

Wildlife? Sure. You won't find any of the big five safari animals here, but the Jozani Forest Reserve is home to the endangered Red Colobus Monkey, a species found nowhere else on Earth that is slowly recovering from near extinction. The reserve is also a hit with watchers of birds and butterflies. Meanwhile Prison Island, one the outer keys in the archipelago, is now a sanctuary for the endangered Aldabra giant tortoise.

Since the 1980s, Zanzibari women have farmed seaweed in the shallow waters off the coast. This part of the ocean was considered the province of women in Tanzanian culture, while the deep sea was solely for fishermen, with the emphasis on men. Many women earned enough money from seaweed to support themselves and even their families. But warmer Indian Ocean temperatures have caused a precipitous drop in the amount of Cottonii seaweed, the most valuable species. Climate change not only affects the environment in Zanzibar, it threatens to return so many women and the families they support to poverty.

Serengeti's Great Migration

Witness the largest movement of mammals on the planet.

Every year, nearly two million wildebeest, half a million gazelles, and 200,000 zebras migrate with their newborn from the plains of Tanzania into Kenya's Maasai Mara game reserve, before circling back to their original starting point. It's one of the world's most transfixing spectacles: a veritable tsunami of massive gnus stretching as far as the eye can see in both directions, moving across the horizon, literally in search of greener pastures. Serengeti means endless plains in the Maasai language and from the middle of the migration, it's easy to see why.

Along the way, the ungulates face multiple perils, including predation from lions, leopards, cheetahs, hyenas, and crocodiles, as well as threats from swift-moving rivers, hunger, thirst, and exhaustion. Only the strongest survive, while as many as a quarter million wildebeest (and tens of thousands of zebras and gazelles) may be killed each year. Those that complete the circuit will have traveled more than 500 miles (800 km). There's no fixed schedule or mapped-out route for the migration. Wildebeest

Plan Your Trip

Location: Northern Tanzania and Southwestern Kenya

Getting There: Most international visitors arrive at Arusha Airport or Kilimanjaro International Airport, then catch bush planes to airstrips along the migration route. The bumpy six-hour drive from Arusha crosses through the Ngorongoro Conservation area—one of the world's best places to see wildlife—prompting many visitors to fly one way and drive the other.

When to Go: During the dry season between June and October, animals are forced to congregate around fewer watering holes, and there's less greenery, making it easier to spot wildlife. There are fewer mosquitoes this time of year, too. January and February is calving season for wildebeest and prime hunting season for predators. There are fewer crowds this time of year. March through May is the rainy season and the worst time to visit, though there may be good viewing opportunities near the Moru Kopjes.

have no natural leaders, but their herd mentality always seems to point them in the direction of water. Zebras and gazelles follow them because they eat different parts of the pasture than the wildebeest.

It's hard to predict exactly where animals will be at different times of year, but certain landmarks are almost always prime viewing spots. One of the most dramatic is along the Mara River separating the Serengeti from the Maasai Mara. Those that

make it down the steep embankment, swim through strong currents past crocodiles, and make it up the far bank without attracting the attention of lions are rewarded with an abundance of fresh grass, clean water, and few places for predators to hide.

Wildebeest populations in both Kenya and Tanzania have dropped precipitously over the past 50 years and will face even more challenges over the next decade, most of them human-induced. New irrigation farms, hydroelectric dams, and diversion of rivers will severely reduce the amount of water that reaches the Serengeti, compounding the effects of natural drought, especially in the dry season. Meanwhile, the human population of the Serengeti ecosystem is expanding rapidly, spurring a corresponding increase in fencing, deforestation, and poaching. And new paved roads through the region threaten to disrupt migration patterns and bring larger-scale tourism and development, which would send the wildebeests the way of the American buffalo.

Volcanoes National Park

Trek through one of the few places you can still see mountain gorillas.

As recently as the 1970s, mountain gorillas were on the brink of extinction. By some estimates, there were no more than 300 of them in the world. Since then, however, thanks to vigorous conservation efforts, the gorilla population has more than tripled to over 1,000. In fact, mountain gorillas are the only species of great apes (other than humans) whose numbers are growing. And tourism has played a critical role in the comeback. Sustainable, carefully managed gorilla-trekking programs have brought in much-needed revenue to protect vital habitats, patrol for poachers, and invest in local communities.

But even with the increase in population, mountain gorillas are still found only in a handful of places in the world: Rwanda, Uganda, and the Democratic Republic of the Congo. Of these three destinations, Rwanda is the best choice for

Plan Your Trip

Location: Rwanda

Getting There: Kigali International Airport welcomes nonstop flights from Amsterdam and Brussels several times a week and is served daily by cities across Africa and the Middle East. The park is about a three-hour drive from the airport.

When to Go: April and May are the rainiest months, so most travelers avoid them. The driest seasons (with the lowest risk of contracting malaria) are June-September and December-February. Although Rwanda is near the equator, the park's high elevation keeps temperatures around 61°F (16°C) year-round.

most travelers. Volcanoes National Park is just a three-hour drive from the international airport in Kigali. By contrast, Uganda's aptly named Bwindi Impenetrable National Park is 310 miles (500 km) over bumpy roads from the capital of Kampala. The terrain in Volcanoes National Park is also more open and more accessible than Uganda's steep, dense jungle, making it more propitious for gorilla sightings. It's also drier—comparatively anyway; no matter where you go, you're trekking through rain forest. While in Rwanda, you can visit the grave of primatologist Dian Fossey, whose 1983 book, *Gorillas in the Mist*, drew attention to the alarming decline in the gorilla population.

The biggest drawback to Volcanoes National Park is the steep price: A permit to visit the Rwanda gorillas is $1,500 per person; Uganda charges $700. Rwanda has pledged to spend at least 10% of tourism revenues on community projects like schools, hospitals, water and sanitation, and retraining poachers as conservation workers.

Despite all the progress of the past half-century, the mountain gorilla's continued existence remains precarious; a war could wipe out nearly the entire population. Habitat loss from encroaching

development is the biggest threat to the gorilla's survival, followed by poaching; gorillas are often killed in traps set by hunters for other animals. And because they are so closely related to humans, gorillas are susceptible to many of the same diseases, including Ebola and COVID. Human contact can be deadly because the animals don't have the immunities that people have. Remember to keep your distance at all times.

Lower Zambezi National Park

Take a safari by canoe or kayak.

The Zambezi River is the star attraction of this wildlife wonderland. In contrast with the roaring thunder of the Zambezi as it cascades over Victoria Falls, the National Park's section of the river is placid enough for canoe and kayak trips ranging from a few hours to a few days. Along the way, paddlers are treated to unequaled views of hippos and Nile crocodiles in the water (crocs are actually less dangerous to humans than hippos, but you'll want to keep your hands and feet inside the boat at all times).

Floating atop the water also gives visitors a different perspective on land-based animals. Overall, there's less diversity here than in some of the more popular safari destinations—no giraffes, cheetahs, or rhinos—but an abundance of buffalo, elephants, and zebra provide ample prey for lions, leopards, and spotted hyenas. Hyenas usually are a sign of leopards: they scavenge for windfall morsels underneath trees where leopards have carted off a fresh kill. African wild dogs, one of the continent's rarest predators, have made a comeback in Lower Zambezi, although sightings are still uncommon.

The combination of land and water makes Lower Zambezi a prime birding destination. More than 350 species have been identified, including waders like egrets and spoonbills, as well as raptors like the osprey or all-black Verreaux's eagle. The elusive Angola pitta, an orange-breasted thrush-like bird, breeds here, but like so many avian species, it is usually sighted only during the wet season.

Lower Zambezi National Park forms a transfrontier conservation area with Zimbabwe's Mana Pools, a UNESCO World Heritage site on the opposite bank of the river. These conservation areas create a broader habitat for animals, which don't recognize international boundaries. Zimbabwe's Chewore Safari Area and Zambia's Chiawa and Rufunsa Game Management Areas abut the national park, doubling the area for wildlife to roam.

Since 2003, conservation groups have been waging a legal battle to prevent a large-scale open pit copper mine within the Lower Zambezi park boundaries. In addition to inhibiting tourism, the mine threatens to contaminate the water supply for communities in Zambia, Zimbabwe, and Mozambique. If the mine is approved, those who make their living from farming, fishing, and tourism will all be negatively impacted. Mining could also undo much of the work of the Lower Zambezi Flagship Species Restoration Project, which is working to restore locally extinct animals like the black rhino and the eland, the world's largest antelope.

Plan Your Trip

Location: Southern Zambia

Getting There: The park entrance is 134 miles (216 km) from Kenneth Kaunda International Airport in the Zambian capital of Lusaka. If you're driving yourself from the airport, be sure to hire a 4×4 vehicle with high clearance for rough roads.

When to Go: Dry season (May-October) features cooler weather, less rain, and thinning vegetation, making it easier to spot wildlife. July and August are the busiest (and consequently most expensive) months to visit.

Victoria Falls

Swim to the edge of a rushing cascade.

Victoria Falls is not the world's tallest waterfall, the widest cataract, or even the one with the greatest volume of water. But it is among the most impressive. The falls span the border between Zambia and Zimbabwe and are flanked by three national parks (two in Zimbabwe and one in Zambia) that preserve the natural beauty of the surrounding area. English explorer David

Livingstone, the first European man to encounter the falls, named the cataract after his queen upon encountering it in 1855. But the locals have always called it Mosi-oa-Tunya, a name that means "The Smoke That Thunders" because of the mist rising off the torrents that fall over the cliffs.

The Zambia side is sometimes known as the wet side, because when the water is at its highest, visitors will get drenched from the spray. It's also the side to visit if you want to take a boat ride to Devil's Pool, a natural rock ledge where you can swim at the edge of the precipice during dry season. It's not as dangerous as most of the photos make it seem. The Zimbabwe side has better views, because the viewpoints are farther away, allowing you to take in the entirety of the spectacle.

You can easily visit both sides in the same day, as long as you have visas for both countries. Walking across the bridge between them allows you to see the falls from both sides or stop in the middle to bungee jump or zipline high above the crocodile-infested Zambezi River. These activities are also much safer than they seem. The less intrepid can take a taxi or a luxury dinner train across the bridge.

The worst drought in more than 100 years slowed the torrential falls to a trickle in 2019, imperiling not only tourism but hydropower from the Kariba dam downstream, which provides electricity to both Zambia and Zimbabwe. The amount of water cascading over the falls always fluctuates with the season, but local officials say they've never seen it so dry. A proposal to build another dam, in the Bakota Gorge, poses a threat to the flora and fauna just below the falls, not to mention the people who live in the surrounding villages.

Plan Your Trip

Location: On the border between Zambia and Zimbabwe

Getting There: Victoria Falls International Airport in Zimbabwe and Livingstone Airport in Zambia both receive flights from Europe and other parts of Africa.

When to Go: This part of Africa is hot year-round. The water level is at its highest from February to May, after the summer rains, so high that mist may often interfere with the view. June through August is the best time to visit if you also want to take a safari. During the dry season from October through November, the Zambian side may be completely dry, and the Zimbabwean side will be mostly bare rock face.

Northwest Namibia

See rare white rhinos and even more elusive black rhinos.

The rhinoceros is the most critically endangered of the Big Five game animals, a list that also includes the lion, leopard, elephant, and Cape buffalo. The Big Five was originally coined by hunters, but contemporary visitors complete their bucket list simply by shooting all five species with cameras. Rhinos are often the last on this list, in part because there are so few of them, and in part because despite their dinosaurian size, they are actually quite hard to spot. Rhinos tend to feed on thick vegetation that hides their hides, and they can go without water for up to five days. Your best bet for seeing one is to visit a watering hole at dusk, when the animals come out to drink.

Southern Africa is a tale of two rhino species. The Southern white rhino is a modern success story. They were thought to be extinct until a small crash (the name for a group of rhinos) was found in 1895 in South Africa. But thanks to conservation efforts, they now number nearly 20,000 and are the only rhino species that is not endangered. The smaller Black rhino, on the other hand, numbered

> ## Plan Your Trip
>
> **Location:** Namibia
>
> **Getting There:** The closest international airport is Hosea Kutako, in Windhoek. From the capital, you can catch a bush plane to airstrips near Etosha and the Damaraland. The paved road from Windhoek to Etosha takes about four hours, but you will need four-wheel drive to get around Damaraland.
>
> **When to Go:** The high season is the dry season between July and October, when animals are easy to spot because there are fewer watering holes. May to August are the coolest months. From October to February, it's both hot and rainy.

in the hundreds of thousands in the 19th century, but their population dwindled to 2,400 by the 1980s. Rhino horn is considered an aphrodisiac in traditional Chinese medicine, creating a market for rhino poaching throughout the world. International trade in rhino horn has been banned since 1977, but a black market still thrives. Poaching is still the biggest threat to all rhinos—more than 1,000 were slaughtered for their horns in 2017 alone—but increased protection and improved management have helped push the black rhino population above 5,000.

Northwest Namibia may be the best place in the world to witness both types of rhinoceros. The region includes Etosha National Park, where you might spot all of the Big Five in a single day, and the Damaraland, an area originally defined by colonizers, which extends west from Etosha to Skeleton Coast National Park on Namibia's Atlantic shore. In a single trip, it's easy to visit both

and even tack on a side trip to the giant red sand dunes of the Namib Desert. Desert Rhino Camp, located in the Palmwag part of the Damaraland, is a partnership between Wilderness Safaris and Save the Rhino Trust. Guests at its eight glamping-style tents accompany Trust conservationists on their rhino-monitoring expeditions in vehicles or on foot. Along the way, they might encounter hyenas, giraffes, springboks, and a collection of 280-million-year-old petrified tree trunks.

Okavango Delta

Share an idyllic desert oasis with thousands of big game animals.

There may be no finer place on earth for an African safari than the Okavango Delta. Sometimes referred to as the Jewel of the Kalahari, this fan-shaped alluvial plain is a true oasis in the desert. What makes the Okavango such a treasure is the water that gives it its lifeblood. Every year, water from the Angolan highlands floods the delta during what would otherwise be the dry season. Animals throughout Southern Africa have learned to migrate to these wetlands when other water sources have dried up.

The result is an Eden-like setting overflowing with animals most people have only seen in zoos or photographs. Elephants (Botswana has more than any other country), giraffes, zebras, rhinos, Cape buffalos, wildebeest, and warthogs coexist in all this abundance. More types of antelopes than you can imagine speed across the landscape, including a species of impala whose M-shaped arches on their rear ends have earned them the name McDonalds; they are literally fast food for the lions, leopards, cheetahs, hyenas, and African wild dogs that have followed the caravan of herbivores to the Okavango. With a little bit of luck (or an especially savvy jeep guide), you might see all Big Five safari animals in a single day.

Botswana has been mindful about limiting the scope of tourism in the delta in the name of sustainability. Most lodges are small affairs with no more than a dozen tents, huts, or bungalows. This makes Botswana safaris more expensive than those in other countries but also much less crowded. Daily (and sometimes nightly) game drives are the best way to see the sights; on a walking safari (accompanied by an armed guide), you'll not just see, but also hear the delta: the patter of birds, the wind through the trees, the elephants tearing down branches to reach higher foliage. Most lodges also offer the opportunity to get out on the water and see elephants swimming among hippos to stay cool in the hot sun.

The Okavango's remote location at the edge of the sparsely populated Kalahari Desert has shielded it from many human-induced threats. It has been

a UNESCO World Heritage site since 2014. But the pristine water that supports the Okavango's amazing diversity of wildlife is increasingly sought by communities upstream in Angola and Botswana. Agriculture doesn't just divert water; it pollutes the rivers with fertilizers that create algae, which reduces the necessary oxygen levels for fish and other underwater life. As rainfall in the region decreases and global temperatures continue to rise, these pressures will be exacerbated, turning more of the Delta into desert.

Plan Your Trip

Location: Botswana

Getting There: The closest international airport of any size is in Maun, the largest town in the Delta. There is regular scheduled service to Maun from Kasane and Gaborone, Botswana's capital, as well as from Cape Town and Johannesburg in South Africa. From Maun, it is possible to drive into the Delta, but most visitors take bush planes to air strips closer to their camps.

When to Go: The best wildlife viewing is between July and October, when the weather is dry, and the flooding is high. Avoid October if you don't like heat. During the rainy season from January to March, some parts of the Delta may be inaccessible.

Cape Floral Region

Drive through a natural botanic garden where two oceans meet.

Africa's southwesternmost tip has been a landmark since sailors renamed the Cape of Storms the Cape of Good Hope on their journeys between the Atlantic and Indian Oceans. Today, it's a beacon for a different reason: its amazing floral diversity. The 9,600 plant species found here are three times the number endemic to the Amazon rain forest. The 4,226-square-mile (1,094,742-hectare) region accounts for less than 0.4% of Africa's land area but is home to 20% of the continent's flora, more than two-thirds of it found nowhere else on Earth. Primary among them are proteas (South Africa's national flower), ericas (with their tubular pink or purple flowers), and the short-lived restios. Species more recognizable to North American gardeners include aloes, geraniums, and gladioli.

To help conserve this floral biodiversity, UNESCO in 2014 conferred World Heritage

Status on eight different protected areas within the region, ranging from Cape Town almost all the way to Lesotho, and added five more sites to the list in 2015. A multiday driving tour is a great way to see them all. Start in Cape Town, one of Africa's most charming cities, and take the gondola up to the top of Table Mountain National Park for outstanding views of the entire region. Then drive south for a loop of the Cape Peninsula that is overflowing with highlights. Look for whales in False Bay from June to October, penguins on the sands of Boulders Beach year-round, wild ostriches as you approach the Cape of Good Hope, and baboons anywhere along the way. Return to Cape Town via Chapman's Peak Drive, a winding road high above the Atlantic coast, with breathtaking views of mountains on one side and Hout Bay on the other.

On day two, head east through the Boland Mountain Complex, itself a collection of five different nature reserves, each with magnificent mountain vistas from hiking trails carpeted with brilliant flowers. Continue south to Hermanus, renowned for its annual flower festival and whale festival (both in September). Return to Cape Town through the Stellenbosch wine region, the Napa Valley of South Africa, known for Cabernet Sauvignons and Chenin Blancs. Or if you have more

time, continue east along the flower route all the way to Groot Winterhoek, where you'll find rock paintings by the San and Khoi people dating back as many as 6,000 years.

Invasive species are the greatest threat to the Cape Floral Region's biodiversity. They usurp water from native plants, increasing the risk of fire, which in turn encourages more invasive species to take root. Climate change is only expected to speed this vicious circle.

Plan Your Trip

Location: South Africa

Getting There: Cape Town International Airport welcomes flights from all over the continent, a few from Europe, and one marathon nonstop (15 hours) from Newark Liberty International.

When to Go: Peak bloom season is South African spring (August-September). June through October are the months for viewing humpback and southern right whales. Peak tourism season is December to February, summer in the southern hemisphere, when the beaches and warm weather beckon vacationers from Africa and beyond.

Madagascar

Visit a world all its own.

BERO/KA
46
TSI/FANA
76

Having separated from the mainland more than 160 million years ago, Madagascar is an African version of the Galapagos, with thousands of plant and animal species that have evolved in isolation for millennia. That isolation also means that few people visit this amazingly diverse land of white sand beaches, pristine coral reefs, lush rainforests, and lemurs, lemurs, lemurs. The Texas-sized island provides shelter for more than 100 species of these monkey-like primates, including the critically endangered, white-furred silky sifaka, one of the rarest mammals on earth.

Lemurs are found almost everywhere in Madagascar, in amazingly varied landscapes. Hikers may spot ring-tailed lemurs and the occasional Verreaux's sifaka in Isalo National Park, sometimes called Madagascar's Grand Canyon. Tropical swimming holes and palm trees pop up among the steep sandstone canyons, a reminder that this region was once underwater.

Fat-trunked baobab trees thrive throughout the island, but nowhere in such great concentration as the Avenue of the Baobabs in Kirindy. The region

Plan Your Trip

Location: More than 700 miles (1,129 km) off the coast of Mozambique in the Indian Ocean

Getting There: Almost all visitors fly into Ivato International Airport in Antananarivo, usually via Dar Es Salaam, Nairobi, or Johannesburg. Air France flies nonstop from Paris.

When to Go: Madagascar's best weather is during the dry winter season (April-October). It's great for sightseeing and whale-watching from June to September. The best wildlife viewing is in November. December-March brings heavy rains and cyclones.

is popular among birders and the Madame Berthe's mouse lemur, the world's smallest primate, is found here and only here. Tsingy de Bemaraha National Park has been a UNESCO World Heritage Site since 1990, for its 11 species of lemurs and its forbidding cathedrals of limestone karst needles. The park and

the adjacent nature reserve are an excellent place to see Madagascar's abundance of orchids—and by extension, vanilla beans, the flower of the orchid plant.

Nosy Be, an archipelago off the northwest coast, is where you'll find idyllic white sand beaches, baby humpback whales from October to December, and the Macaco lemur. Visitors can swim with whale sharks, the largest fish in the world. Off the southeast coast, the protected bays and inlets of Ile St. Marie once drew pirate ships, wrecks of which snorkelers and scuba divers can explore. Humpback whales populate the waters from June to September, while fat-tailed dwarf lemurs inhabit the trees year-round.

Slash-and-burn agriculture has deforested as much as 90% of Madagascar's land area, destroying habitats for its unique flora and fauna. Logging of ebony and rosewood poses a serious risk to the forests that remain, while poaching threatens extinction for several species of chameleons and endangered lemurs. The Rainforests of the Atsinanana, a designation that includes six different national parks, have been a UNESCO World Heritage Site since 2007, and on UNESCO's List in Danger since 2010.

Seychelles

Stroll a different deserted beach every day.

This archipelago of more than 100 islands in the Indian Ocean is notable for multiple reasons: they're the only oceanic islands made of granite, and at 700 million years of age, they're among the world's oldest islands. But let's be honest: the reason most people dream about visiting Africa's least populated country is the beaches: miles and miles of virtually empty snow-white sands with just enough palm trees to provide shade on hot days. There's a different beach for every day of the year, and one to fit every traveler's preference. All the beaches are public, and if that's not enough seclusion, you can rent a private island.

The mile-long (1.6-km) Anse Intendance, on the main island of Mahé, is surprisingly uncrowded for a strand so close to the capital. Its big swells make

Plan Your Trip

Location: In the Indian Ocean, about 940 miles (1,512 km) east of Kenya

Getting There: Seychelles International Airport is in the capital, Victoria, on the main island of Mahé. Most flights connect through Dubai or Nairobi. Interisland flights and ferries connect Mahé with the other islands in the archipelago.

When to Go: The Seychelles are warm and tropical year-round. The cooler and drier season from June through September is also the most crowded and most expensive time to visit. The best snorkeling and diving, however, is during the rainy season from October to April.

it more popular for surfing than swimming. On La Digue Island, the oversize granite boulders of Anse Source d'Argent are familiar to viewers of movies like *Cast Away* and *Crusoe*. Families love its calm, shallow waters. The coral reefs off Anse Lazio, on Praslin Island, attract snorkelers and divers.

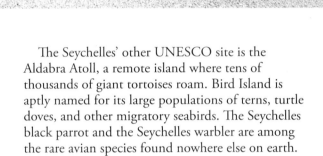

Praslin is also the location of Vallée de Mai, one of two UNESCO World Heritage sites in Seychelles. A local myth alleges the Vallée is the real-life location of the Garden of Eden, a claim buttressed by the forests of endangered Coco de Mer trees, whose seeds come in both male and female varieties, each explicitly suggestive of gender. These palms bear the world's largest nuts, weighing up to 66 pounds (30 kg).

The Seychelles' other UNESCO site is the Aldabra Atoll, a remote island where tens of thousands of giant tortoises roam. Bird Island is aptly named for its large populations of terns, turtle doves, and other migratory seabirds. The Seychelles black parrot and the Seychelles warbler are among the rare avian species found nowhere else on earth.

Coral bleaching events over the past 25 years have devastated the Seychelles' reefs. The El Niño year of 1998 killed 90% of the live coral around the archipelago. In 2019, ocean temperatures reached 88°F (31°C), causing another die-off. The loss of coral doesn't just harm marine life and ruin vacations for snorkelers. In addition to housing more than 25% of the world's diversity, healthy reefs protect shorelines against erosion. In the Seychelles in particular, as reefs have degraded, coastal flooding has increased, causing some of those beautiful beaches to wash away.

MIDDLE EAST

Petra

Walk through a "Lost City" emerging from the cliffs.

It seems a little ironic that a city dating back to the 4th century BCE would be considered one of the "New" Seven Wonders of the World (a designation bestowed by a Swiss foundation in 2007, based on votes from tens of millions of people worldwide). But that may have to do with the fact that Petra essentially disappeared for more than 1,000 years before Swiss explorer Johann Ludwig Burckhardt rediscovered it in 1812.

Once the capital of the Nabataean Arab world, and a major trading center for frankincense, myrrh, and other spices, Petra fell to the Roman Empire in 106 CE. A major earthquake in 363 CE destroyed much of the city but left intact an impressive array of structures literally carved out of the surrounding red sandstone cliffs. It has been a UNESCO World Heritage Site since 1985.

Plan Your Trip

Location: Jordan

Getting There: Petra is about a two-hour drive from King Hussein International Airport in Aqaba or a 2.5-hour drive from Queen Alia International Airport in Amman.

When to Go: April or May are the best months, combining low rainfall and temperatures much cooler than during the sweltering Arab summer or the chilly desert winter.

An easy 2.5-mile (4-km) path links all the major marvels of the Rose Red City, starting at the Bab Al Siq (home to a visitor center), the Obelisk

Tomb, and four pyramids. Next up is The Dam, a testament to the Nabataeans' engineering skills. Renovated in 1964 by Jordan's government using the same methods as the original architects, the dam successfully protected the city by channeling floodwaters into tunnels and underground cisterns.

On hot days, the Siq, a ¾-mile (1.2-km) gorge through the rock, is one of the coolest places to be. Its high walls keep the narrow canyon floor (no wider than 10 feet [3 meters] in some places) shrouded in shade. The Siq connects The Dam to The Treasury (a.k.a. Al Khazneh), perhaps the most photographed place in all of Jordan. From a distance, the Treasury looks like somebody painted the New York Stock Exchange building onto the surrounding sandstone (which may be how it got its name; archaeologists still aren't sure what the building's original purpose was). Look a little closer, and you'll find statues, friezes, and a funerary urn (where a pharaoh's treasure is secreted, according to legend) sculpted into the facade.

Although Petra has survived for more than 20 centuries, its future may not be assured for the next one. Sandstone's soft nature made it easy to sculpt, but it is vulnerable to erosion. Countless fingers of tourists touching the Treasury, for example, have worn down its surface by 1.5 inches (3.8 cm), while the hooves of camels and donkeys have eaten away at the stonework paths. That doesn't mean you shouldn't visit, however. Just make sure to tread lightly and keep your hands to yourself.

Jerusalem's Old City

Explore the birthplace of three major religions.

For nearly half the world's population, history begins here. This 247-acre (1-sq.-km) tract is sacred to all three Abrahamic religions (Judaism, Christianity, and Islam) for different reasons. For Jews, the Western Wall (a.k.a. the Wailing Wall, or Kotel, as it is known in Hebrew) is the last remaining section of the former Jewish Temple. This is where you'll find people writing prayers on pieces of paper and tucking them into the cracks in the wall.

Just beyond the Wall, in the Muslim quarter, the golden Dome of the Rock sits atop the Temple Mount, known to Muslims as al-Haram al-Sharif. One of the oldest extant structures in Islamic architecture, the Dome marks the location where Muslims believe the prophet Muhammad began his journey to heaven. The Foundation Stone at the center of the temple is believed to be the site where Abraham offered to sacrifice his son to God.

The Christian quarter of the old city is home to the Church of the Holy Sepulchre, a complex that includes the two holiest sites in Christianity: the location where Jesus was crucified and that of his empty tomb. Within the church itself are the last four stations of the Cross of the via Dolorosa.

For an overview (literally) of the entire old city, take the Ramparts Walk atop the fortifications built during the 16th century by the Ottoman emperor Suleiman the Magnificent. From Jaffa Gate on the western side of the city, you can walk clockwise around the Christian quarter before crossing into

the Muslim quarter, and descend at the Lion's Gate, near the Dome of the Rock. Or go counterclockwise past the Armenian quarter and the Jewish quarter before exiting the parapet near Wailing Wall Plaza. The northern (clockwise) route is the longer of the two, but each is less than 2 miles (3 km). There is a small fee to enter the ramparts walk.

A UNESCO World Heritage site since 1981, the old city has been considered a site in danger almost continuously ever since. According to UNESCO, the direst threats to Jerusalem's cultural heritage, authenticity, and integrity include ongoing archaeological excavations by Israel under the old city, and a proposed cable car system that would significantly change the character of the East Jerusalem skyline.

Plan Your Trip

Location: Jerusalem

Getting There: Tel Aviv's Ben Gurion International is the closest airport, about 25 miles away from the old city.

When to Go: The best weather is during April and May, when days are warm but not hot, and nights are cool but not cold. But check the dates of Passover and Easter, when prices and crowds both surge. Tourism is lowest in October and November, except when Yom Kippur or Ramadan happen to fall during this period.

Dead Sea

Float in buoyant water at the planet's lowest point.

Ten times as salty as the ocean, the Dead Sea gets its name from the fact that nothing can survive in its waters—no fish, no marine animals, no seaweed, nothing. "Sea," however, is a misnomer; because water flows in but doesn't flow out, it's a lake. People have been visiting the Dead Sea for millennia in search of its reported healing properties, including the warm, high mineral content of the water itself, as well as the warm, pollen-free air in the lowest place on earth (1,412 ft/431 m below sea level).

Dead Sea salt is harvested for use in beauty products, but the nutrient-rich mud on the shores may be better than any spa treatment. And after you rinse off, you can float in water so buoyant you can read a book. The mud has a slightly sulfuric smell, but the beautiful, azure water does not. Resort hotels and spas line both the Israel and Jordan sides of the sea, many with their own beaches, lifeguards, and shade structures. (You'll want to avail yourself of the latter; temperatures here often top 100°F, or 38°C.)

Plan Your Trip

Location: On the border between Israel, Jordan, and the Palestinian territories

Getting There: Queen Alia International Airport in Amman, Jordan, is about an hour's drive from the northeastern shore. Ben Gurion International in Tel Aviv, Israel, is a two-hour drive from the popular resorts at Ein Gedi, on the western shore.

When to Go: November through March. Temperatures are uncomfortably hot the rest of the year.

What's the urgency to visiting something that's already "dead"? The water level here is falling faster than ever: more than 3 feet (1.2 meters) per year, according to Israel's Ministry of Environmental Protection. The Dead Sea is nearly 1,000 feet (304 meters) deep, so even at current rates, it

would take centuries for the sea to dry up. But its breadth is now half what it was in 1976. As the sea has receded, it has left behind sinkholes, more than 6,000 of them at last count, many of them big enough to swallow a house.

Climate change isn't directly responsible for the impending environmental disaster; human activity is. Water from the Jordan River that formerly flowed into the Dead Sea is now being diverted by Syria, Jordan, and Israel as drinking water. And mineral extraction companies in both Israel and Jordan continue to pump Dead Sea water into evaporation ponds to create potash.

Sphinx and the Great Pyramid of Giza

Visit the only remaining wonder of the Ancient World.

Whose bucket list doesn't include a visit to the Great Pyramid of Giza? It's the oldest of the Seven Wonders of the Ancient World and the only one that is still intact. And the superlatives don't stop there. For nearly 4,000 years (from its completion around 2600 BCE until England's Lincoln Cathedral was built in 1311), it was the tallest building in the world.

Even today, scientists aren't sure how the pyramids were built. What they do know is that the largest of the three major pyramids was built by the Pharaoh Khufu (you'll sometimes hear it called the Pyramid of Khufu). The next-largest necropolis was erected by his son, Pharaoh Khafre, who also commissioned the Sphinx statue that stands sentry outside its entrance. The Sphinx was carved from a single piece of limestone in the Giza bedrock, which was exposed when workers quarried the blocks used to build the pyramids. The third and smallest tomb was erected by Pharaoh Menkaure around 2490 BCE.

You can't go inside the Sphinx unless you're an archaeologist on assignment, but you can enter the pyramids (separate admission fees apply for each tomb). Note that the stairways into the interior are quite narrow, and the temperature inside can be even hotter than outside.

For some visitors, seeing the pyramids from atop a camel is a lifelong dream attained, allowing them to imagine they are walking in the footsteps of the ancients. For others, a camel ride feels like a tourist trap involving unpleasant bargaining over prices and smelly, underfed animals. Visitors are similarly divided about the sound and light show that plays out here after sunset. Fans say it's an unforgettable experience well worth the price of the ticket. Detractors say it's a cheesy production that you can see just as well for free from your hotel room or other locations in Giza.

The Cairo metropolitan area sprawls closer to Giza every year, bringing with it urban

problems like trash, air pollution, vandalism, and kitschy tourist shops a stone's throw from the pyramids. But perhaps the greatest concern is rising groundwater levels from irrigation canals and leaking sewage from the new suburbs. Some preservationists believe the groundwater rise is weakening the very foundation of the Sphinx, and wicking up to its surface, where evaporation causes the limestone to flake off, bit by bit.

Plan Your Trip

Location: Egypt

Getting There: Giza is about a 45-minute drive from Cairo, or about an hour from Cairo International Airport.

When to Go: Temperatures are coolest between December and February, but this is also the most popular time to visit. The shoulder seasons (March–April and October–November) have smaller crowds and weather that isn't yet stiflingly hot.

Memphis

Witness the evolution of pyramid construction.

Egypt's first capital city is older than the Great Pyramids at Giza, and a half-hour farther from Cairo by car. But visitors love it because it's a lot less crowded than Egypt's main attraction—and because you can climb on several structures. A visit to Memphis usually involves three different stops. The first is the village of Mit-Rahineh, home to an outdoor museum of stumps of pillars and foundations of long-fallen buildings. A massive, prone statue of Ramesses II and an alabaster sphinx round out the highlights here.

Saqqara, a 20-minute drive to the west, is the location of Memphis's necropolis, built some 70 years before the Great Pyramid at Giza, making it the world's oldest such structure. It's known as the Step Pyramid because it looks like a cross between an oversized triangular layer cake and a ziggurat. It's easy to imagine it as a rough draft for the smooth-sided pyramids that would follow.

Plan Your Trip

Location: Egypt

Getting There: Memphis is about an hour south of Cairo by car.

When to Go: Late October to early April. Temperatures are uncomfortably hot the rest of the year. Check the calendar to see if Ramadan falls within these months. Muslims fast during Ramadan's daylight hours, causing many businesses and services to slow down or change hours.

In Dahshur, the Bent Pyramid serves as an additional lesson in construction techniques. Its bottom half is canted at a steep 54 degrees, but about halfway up, the angle levels off to 43 degrees.

Archaeologists believe the change in slope was critical in preventing the building from collapsing. The proof of this theory is seen in the Red Pyramid, built 50 years later, which follows the 43-degree angle from top to bottom. Both pyramids offer visitors the opportunity to climb up the outside and then descend into the belly of the building (via a long, steep, claustrophobia-inducing tunnel).

Memphis faces the usual threats from increasing urbanization, including pollution and rising groundwater. But what really worries preservationists are two new eight-lane highways through the surrounding desert, which archaeologists fear will damage still-to-be-unearthed ancient treasures and encourage antiquities thefts. UNESCO, which declared Memphis, the Pyramids, and most of the Giza plateau a World Heritage site in 1979, successfully blocked the construction of these roads in 1995. But the projects were revived in preparation for the opening of the Grand Egyptian Museum, the world's largest archaeological museum.

Cedars of Lebanon

Walk through forests of 1,000-year-old trees.

Cedar trees are so integral to Lebanon that they appear on the country's flag and its currency and are referenced in the national anthem as a symbol of immortality. The ancient Egyptians used Lebanese cedars for their sarcophagi, and the Phoenicians built their ships from cedar.

The most famous copse is a reserve of 2,100 trees located high on the slope of Mount al-Makmal in northern Lebanon, nicknamed the Cedars of God and referenced in the Mesopotamian-era Epic of Gilgamesh. None of the current trees date that far back, but some are more than 1,000 years old. They have been protected against deforestation by fences since 1876, and by UNESCO, which declared the reserve a World Heritage Site in 1998.

Plan Your Trip

Location: Lebanon

Getting There: Tannourine Cedars Forest Nature Reserve is about a two-hour drive from Beirut, slightly longer from Beirut-Rafic Hariri International Airport

When to Go: Spring (March–May) is the ideal time of year to visit Lebanon, halfway between the rainy winter and the scorching summer. Summer is high season, when many of the country's artistic and cultural festivals take place. Always check the calendar for when Ramadan falls before visiting. Muslims fast during Ramadan's daylight hours, causing many businesses and services to slow down or change hours.

Unfortunately, there's little available land around the reserve to plant additional trees.

The Tannourine Cedars Forest Nature Reserve, also in northern Lebanon, has the country's densest concentration of cedars. The short walking trails through the reserve are an exceptional way to see (and smell) the majesty of these legendary conifers.

In the 21st century, Lebanon's cedar forests have been ravaged by fire, whose frequency and intensity have soared. Rising temperatures have also brought infestations of web-spinning sawflies, which feast on cedar buds, killing trees before they get a chance to flourish. The Beirut government and private agencies alike have attempted to offset declining cedar populations by planting more trees wherever they can. But cedars can take up to 50 years to mature, setting up a race against climate change's ticking clock.

ASIA

Maldives

Choose one island paradise or hop among hundreds of choices.

Maldives has so many atolls—more than 1,000 in all, 200 of them inhabited—that dozens of luxury resorts each claim their own private island. That makes the country immensely popular (albeit expensive) for honeymooners seeking to spend some alone time together. Overwater bungalows are nearly as common as palm trees along the thousands of miles of silky, white-sand beaches. The underwater hotel room at the Conrad Maldives Rangali Island, on the other hand, is the only one of its kind in the Maldives, although several resorts have wine cellars, restaurants, or spas where guests can venture under the sea without getting wet.

Naturally, activities here revolve around the crystal-clear emerald waters that surround the Maldives in every direction. Many islands are within a short swim of a reef, so snorkelers and divers can explore right from shore. For a deeper dive—literally—check out the *Maldive Victory*, which sank after crashing on the Hulhulé Reef in 1981.

If you want to swim with whale sharks, base yourself on South Ari Atoll, especially between June and September during the migration of the world's largest fish. Surfers favor Huvadhoo Atoll or Gan Island for their reliable (and reliably uncrowded) breaks. The main island of Malé is the launching point for fishing charters in search of barracuda, red bass, and the occasional yellowfin tuna. Or you can sample a little bit of everything by island-hopping on a liveaboard, a.k.a. a boat and breakfast. More intimate than a cruise, these houseboats, yachts, or catamarans accommodate just a handful of guests, and can be staffed with a chef, a surfing instructor, a dive master, or even a masseuse.

While relaxing in paradise, it's easy to forget that the Maldives are a Muslim country. Outside of the vacation resorts, alcohol is not permitted, and conservative dress is required (no shorts or swimwear).

The Maldives may be the country most vulnerable to rising oceans. More than 80% of its land area sits less than 3 feet (1 meter) above sea level; fresh water sources are constantly at risk of being inundated by salt water. The country made

headlines in 2008 when it bought land in Australia in preparation for the day when its atolls become uninhabitable. Since then, it has erected seawalls around its existing population centers, and built Hulhumalé, an artificial island filled with high-rise apartment buildings.

Plan Your Trip

Location: Indian Ocean, about 500 miles (800 km) southwest of Sri Lanka

Getting There: There is no direct service from North America to Velana International Airport. But there are nonstop flights from most European capitals, the Middle East, and southern Asia.

When to Go: The Maldives span the equator, with temperatures rarely dropping below 75°F (24°C). The dry season (January-April) has lower humidity. December is a popular time of year to visit but can be rainy.

Taj Mahal

Book a passage to India before this architectural jewel collapses.

India's most recognizable building was commissioned by the Mughal emperor Shah Jahan in 1632 to honor his wife, Mumtaz Mahal, who died giving birth to the couple's 14th child. Nearly 400 years later, the white marble palace still stands as the world's finest extant example of Mughal architecture, which blends Indian, Persian, and Islamic styles.

A UNESCO World Heritage site since 1983, the mausoleum is India's top tourist attraction, drawing more than six million visitors every year. That's

more than 20,000 people a day, so expect crowds no matter when you visit. In general, it's best to go early in the day (especially in hot months), but there's usually a queue starting about an hour before the gates open.

Unlike so many bucket-list attractions, Taj Mahal does not disappoint. Many visitors find it even more impressive in person than in pictures. The crowds notwithstanding, the mausoleum is a peaceful place, surrounded by 42 acres (17 hectares) of gardens and pedestrian plazas. Cars are not allowed within 1,600 feet (500 meters) of the grounds.

Once pearly white, the Taj is now a yellow-gray, thanks to acid rain and rampant air pollution. Critics say the Indian government has done a poor job of maintenance, deferring some needed repairs for too long, and making a hash out of others. Case in point: mudpacks were applied to the exterior in 2017, in the hopes that the poultices would draw out acid from the marble, but if anything, the treatment made the discoloration even worse.

India's Supreme Court chastised government officials in 2018 for letting the Taj deteriorate. "If such an indifference of officials continues," the Court said in a statement, "then authorities should demolish it." That's unlikely to happen any time soon, but the mausoleum might fall on its own

without effective intervention. The Yamuna River, which once reflected the Taj's magnificence in its glittering blue waters, is now nearly dry, and filled with sewage and other pollution. The lack of water in the river also threatens to erode the building's wooden foundation, which needs moisture to avoid drying out.

Plan Your Trip

Location: Agra, India

Getting There: There are no international flights to Agra. Visitors from overseas can catch a two-hour flight from Mumbai or a two-hour train ride from New Delhi. It is also possible to drive or take a bus from Delhi.

When to Go: March or October. The average temperature tops 100°F (38°C) from April through June. Monsoon season (July-September) brings torrential rains. Winter (November-February) is dry and cool, but fog often obscures views. So can crowds, as this is high tourism season. Taj Mahal is closed on Fridays year-round. The site opens 30 minutes before sunrise and closes 30 minutes before sunset. When the moon is full (except during Ramadan), Taj Mahal opens for nighttime viewing at half-hour intervals from 8:30 PM to 12:30 AM.

Bandhavgarh and Kanha National Parks

There's no better place to see tigers.

Madhya Pradesh is known as India's "Tiger State," a distinction it earned by reporting 526 of the critically endangered cats within its borders. That's out of a total of less than 4,000 worldwide, according to the World Wildlife Fund. Unfortunately, Madhya Pradesh also had the highest number of tiger fatalities (43) of any Indian state in 2021. Many of those deaths were caused by electrified traps, used by hunters to catch wild boars; poaching and poisoning also played a role.

Tigers have lost an estimated 95% of their historical range to logging, farming, and other human activity. As their natural habitat dwindles, so too does their prey, forcing them to stray from protected sanctuaries in search of food. This often puts them in conflict with people, a battle tigers usually lose.

Plan Your Trip

Location: Madhya Pradesh, India

Getting There: The closest airport is in Jabalpur, a scenic four-hour drive from either park. The parks form a rough triangle with Jabalpur, persuading many visitors to stop at both in a single trip. There are no international flights to Jabalpur, but you can catch a flight from cities within India, including Mumbai and Delhi.

When to Go: October-February is the best time to visit either park. Summer (March-June) can be unbearably hot, while monsoon season (July-September) brings heavy rains.

Even in the state with the most tigers, odds of seeing a tiger in the wild are long. To maximize your chances, go on a photo safari of Bandhavgarh National Park. The park is known as the land of the white tiger, because the last time one of these felines was recorded was here, back in 1951. Declared a national park in 1968, Bandhavgarh's compact 41 square miles (105 sq. km) are home to more than 50 wild tigers.

In addition to tigers, visitors may spot leopards, langur monkeys, and several species of deer. Bandhavgarh is also a birder's paradise: the park's official list includes more than 250 species, but visitors have recorded as many as 350, including plum-headed parakeets, orange-headed thrushes, rock pigeons, and three different species of vultures. The epicenter of the park is Bandhavgarh Fort, India's oldest. Its ramparts are a favored bird-watching perch.

Kanha National Park, by contrast, is one of India's largest national parks, with a tiger population similar to Bandhavgarh's, but spread out over 362 square miles (940 sq. km). Kanha's stunning landscapes were the inspiration for Rudyard Kipling's *The Jungle Book*. You probably won't have a black panther like Bagheera watching over you, but you might encounter bison, hyenas, leopards, and sloth bears that remind you of Baloo.

Kanha is abundant with barasingha, sometimes known as swamp deer, a species once on the verge of extinction but now thriving in the meadows sprinkled among Kanha's teak and bamboo forests. During rutting season (September-November), males bugle to attract mates, so it's likely that you'll hear them before you see them. Assuming a tiger doesn't hear them first, that is.

Golden Temple

Make a pilgrimage before its sheen has literally worn off.

Known in Punjabi as Harmandir Sahib, India's Golden Temple is the holiest shrine in the Sikh faith. Each year, millions of Sikhs make pilgrimages to the city of Amritsar to pay their respects to the Guru Granth Sahib, the holiest book in the Sikh tradition.

But you don't have to be Sikh to enter this sacred shrine. The temple's four entrances (on the north, south, east, and west sides) welcome visitors from all four corners of the world. There is only one route, however, to the temple's inner sanctum sanctorum, a metaphor for the one true path to enlightenment.

A moat surrounds the temple, making the building appear to hover above the water. Guru Ram Das built the pool in 1577, and its waters are considered holy. Bathing in the pool is said to purify one's karma, and plenty of visitors do exactly that. Others take home a bottle of the holy water.

The Guru Granth Sahib is treated like a living person. At dawn each day, it is removed from its bedroom and carried on a palanquin to the sanctum, where it is opened to a random page. The words from that page are read aloud and revisited by pilgrims throughout the day. At dusk, the book is literally put to bed for the night. Sunset may be the best time to visit, as it allows you to arrive during daylight, watch the return of the holy book to its bedroom, and see the temple lit up in blue light as night approaches. Visitors must cover their heads; refrain from eating, drinking, and smoking; and treat the campus as a place of quiet reflection.

There are several non-gilded buildings within the temple complex, including a community kitchen known as a langar, which dishes out 75,000 free vegetarian meals to hungry people every day. All food is donated, and the labor of cooking and serving is performed by volunteers.

Over its 440-year history, the Golden Temple has been sacked and rebuilt several times. In the 21st century, though, it is falling to a foe of an entirely

different kind: India's notorious air pollution, which is taking the sheen off the gold-plated walls and dome, leaving them a dull gray. Sadly, there isn't much to be done about it short of replacing all of the plating, a solution that was already tried from 1995-99. The government has banned burning trash and restricted traffic near the temple, but the location—near a major bus terminal and a 25-acre (10-hectare) garbage dump—makes fighting pollution an uphill battle.

Plan Your Trip

Location: Amritsar, Punjab, India

Getting There: Amritsar's airport has nonstop flights from most of India's major cities, and from London and Birmingham, UK; Singapore; Abu Dhabi and Dubai, UAE; and Doha, Qatar. The train ride from Delhi is about six hours.

When to Go: Northern India has hot summers and cold winters. The months in between (February and March or October and November) are ideal times to visit. Monsoon season starts in July and lasts through September. In winter (December-January), fog can often delay flights.

Jaipur, India

The Pink City is red hot.

The capital of India's Rajasthan state has been known as the Pink City since 1876, when Maharaja Ram Singh had every building in the city painted the color of hospitality in advance of a visit by Queen Victoria's son, Albert Edward (later Emperor of India as King Edward VII). A year later, the maharaja passed a law requiring all future edifices be pink as well. The result is a city bathed in shades from mauve to magenta.

The city has been a UNESCO World Heritage Site since 2019, not just for its uniform hues, but also for the ingenious urban planning that made it a center for trade. Jaipur was laid out along a grid, with large public squares at prominent intersections. The state built most of the main markets, shops, and temples along the major streets, giving the city a unified façade that became even more singular when painted pink.

Two of Jaipur's top attractions—the Amer Fort and the Jantar Mantar—are also UNESCO sites. The fort's centerpiece is the palace of Raja Man Singh, who built this oldest section from 1574

Plan Your Trip

Location: Rajasthan, northwestern India

Getting There: Jaipur Airport receives flights from most major cities in India, as well as nonstop service from Bangkok, Thailand, and Dubai, UAE.

When to Go: The temperature is pleasantly warm between November and the end of February. It is often uncomfortably hot and muggy the rest of the year.

to 1599, with a different bedroom for each of his 12 wives. Over the next 150 years, subsequent rulers expanded the complex to include four courtyards, a garden, a temple, extensive ramparts, and ornate gates. The fort is sometimes called the Amber Palace because of the tawny color of the sandstone and marble buildings. The fort is located about 7 miles (11 km) northeast of Jaipur proper, standing sentry above Maota Lake.

The Jantar Mantar, meanwhile, is a unique collection of 20-some astronomical instruments the

size of houses, all designed to detect the positions of the sun and stars with the naked eye. Built in the early 18th century by Maharaja Jai Singh II, it is the most comprehensive and best-preserved example of India's historic observatories.

Jaipur is one of India's hottest cities, in more ways than one. From April to July, the mercury averages close to 100°F (38°C). As the city's fast-growing population expands, concrete, asphalt, and dense clusters of buildings replace natural vegetation and bodies of water, creating what's known as heat islands. The temperature in Churu, 12 miles (20 km) north of Jaipur, hit 122°F (50°C) in 2020. Moreover, natural streams that once trickled down from the mountains to cool the city are now often blocked by garbage in rapidly expanding outskirts.

Mount Everest

Climb on top of the world … or a step just below it.

WAY TO M.T.
EVEREST B.C.

The highest point on earth inspires awe, even for those who have never climbed more than a flight of stairs. Humans have attempted to summit Everest for more than a century, and in the 70 years since Edmund Hillary and Tenzing Norgay first accomplished the feat in 1953, more than 6,000 have succeeded.

That doesn't mean it's easy. Everest isn't the toughest mountain to climb, but it still requires mountaineering skills, peak fitness levels, months of preparation, and a lot of money. A typical expedition costs around $50,000, putting it well beyond the reach of most vacationers.

A trip to Everest Base Camp, however, is somewhat more manageable, requiring neither supplemental oxygen nor technical climbing skills. This trek ends at 17,600 feet (5,364 meters), an elevation where most summit attempts are just getting started. But it offers many of the same life-changing experiences as a full ascent: breathtaking vistas, glacial lakes framed by jagged mountain peaks, dense alpine forests, glacial moraines, and cultural exchange with the local Sherpa people.

From the Nepalese village of Lukla, the 40-mile (65-km) trail to Everest Base Camp is

Plan Your Trip

Location: Northeastern Nepal, near the Chinese border

Getting There: Tenzing-Hillary airport in Lukla, Nepal, is the gateway to Everest. The steep descent onto its short runway is an adventure all its own, made more challenging during adverse weather. To get to Lukla, take a connecting flight from Kathmandu's Tribhuvan International Airport, which receives nonstop flights from Istanbul, half a dozen cities in the Middle East, and most Asian capitals.

When to Go: April and May are the best months for attempting a full summit of Everest. If you're only going as far as base camp, skies are generally clearer in October and November.

marked well enough for most trekkers to go it alone. But most visitors prefer to hire a local guide and/or porter for assistance and expertise at a reasonable price. For an even more seamless trip, a trekking outfitter will take care of flights, accommodations, meals, insurance, porters, and

a guide who can recognize the signs of altitude sickness.

The round-trip journey to Base Camp and back takes about 12 days: 8 going up and 4 coming down. That works out to no more than five miles a day, but the elevation gain is perhaps the biggest challenge. Lukla is at 9,383 feet (2,860 meters), an altitude at which some people start having trouble breathing. At 14,000 feet, the air holds only 50% of the oxygen as at sea level, so even light exercise feels like an uphill climb.

Everest is more popular than ever, but it might not be accessible forever. Himalayan glaciers are melting at an alarming rate. Ice that took 2,000 years to form has disappeared in just the past 25 years. Territory once covered by snow and ice are now glacial lakes large enough to row a boat across, or worse, covered in tons of human waste left behind by past expeditions (not to mention corpses of those who failed in their summit attempts). For communities living downstream, the melting glaciers mean more avalanches and more frequent flooding in the short term, and less water for drinking, irrigation, and hydropower in the long-term.

Bhutan

Take a trip to the happiness place on earth.

"Why Is Everyone Going to Bhutan?" a *New York Times* headline wondered back in 2005. At the time, "everyone" meant a total of 9,000 people a year, or about the same number as arrive in Las Vegas every hour. But for Bhutan, a landlocked country in the Himalayas that didn't allow outsiders to cross its borders until 1972, it was a veritable onslaught.

Visitation numbers have increased exponentially to about 250,000 annually (most from India and China), but you needn't worry that Bhutan has become a tourist trap. The country's official state policy promotes "conditions that will enable the pursuit of Gross National Happiness." Buddhism, the national religion, helps explain Bhutanese happiness, or at least contentment. Furthermore, the nation has no traffic lights, one of the highest vaccination rates in the world, and a long list of colorful festivals.

Bhutan's mountain scenery rivals that of India or Nepal, but summiting its peaks is forbidden, so as not to disturb the spirits that inhabit the mountaintops. However, you're welcome to hike

or bike through mountains of virgin forests, kayak or raft down glacier-fed rivers, or trek through an incredibly biodiverse habitat for snow leopards, red pandas, elephants, rhinos, and hundreds of species of birds. The most popular attraction in this placid nation is a 17th-century monastery, nicknamed the Tiger's Nest. Perched on a high cliff 10,000 feet

Plan Your Trip

Location: In the Himalayas between northern India and southern China

Getting There: Bhutan's only international airport is in Paro; it receives nonstop flights from Bangkok, Singapore, and Kathmandu, as well as Delhi, Mumbai, and a few other cities in India.

When to Go: Spring (March-May) and fall (September-November) have the best weather and are considered high season. The "Minimum Daily Package" rate set by the government is lower in winter (which can be cold and snowy) and summer, when monsoons bring humidity and heavy rain.

(3,048 meters) above the city of Paro, it can be reached only by a four-hour round-trip hike.

To deter the kind of mass tourism that could threaten Bhutan's appealing serenity, the country has implemented a campaign of high-value, low-volume visitation. A "Minimum Daily Package" requires visitors to spend $200 ($250 in high season) on each day of their stay. That may seem like a lot, but it includes everything from accommodations and meals to transportation, expert guides, entry fees, and trekking permits.

Even with the emphasis on high-end tourism, the influx of visitors can't help but have an impact on the most popular spots. Old hands say the country has lost some of its charm from the days before "everyone" started visiting. The greater threat to this kingdom isn't crowds but climate change. Bhutan is carbon-negative overall, but its conservation efforts can't begin to counteract the damage caused by other countries. Higher temperatures are already accelerating snowmelt in the Himalayas, which will increase flooding and landslides. Bhutan is also heavily dependent on hydroelectric power, which will also be affected by changing weather patterns.

Angkor

Wander through the remains of a 900-year-old city.

The world's largest religious monument sprawls across more than 400 acres (163 hectares) and was for a time the epicenter of a thriving city with the geographic size of Berlin and a population the size of Boston (700,000). Originally built in the 12th century as a Hindu temple dedicated to the god Vishnu, Angkor slowly transformed to a place of Buddhist worship. The surrounding jungle reclaimed most of the site after the Khmer empire fell in 1431, but it was never completely abandoned.

Today, the main temple and some 70 other structures stand as a testament to the ingenuity of the architects. Thousands of laborers quarried huge blocks of sandstone from the nearby Kulen Mountains and used elephants to transport them to the site. There, Khmer artists carved intricate bas-relief Hindu subjects into the facades. Every window and door opening is a perfect 90-degree angle, an indication of how much geometry the artisans knew nearly 1,000 years ago.

Angkor Wat, which means Temple City in Khmer, is the first stop for most visitors. Surrounded by a moat, it's the national symbol of Cambodia. But it's far from the only attraction here. Ta Prohm offers a glimpse of what French explorer

Plan Your Trip

Location: Siem Riep, Cambodia

Getting There: Angkor International Airport is just 5 miles (8 km) from the gateway town of Siem Reap, where most hotels are located. There are no direct flights from the U.S. or Europe; connect through a major city in Asia, such as Hanoi, Singapore, Kuala Lumpur, or Hong Kong.

When to Go: Cambodia is hot year-round and rainy from May through October. High season is the dry season from November to April. November has the best combination of weather and lower prices on airfare and hotel rooms.

Henri Mouhout saw when he "rediscovered" the site in 1860: a land where fig, banyan, and kapok trees envelop the buildings. Ta Prohm is known as the "Tomb Raider" temple, because it's featured in a scene from the 2001 film *Lara Croft: Tomb Raider*.

Good walking shoes are a must for exploring Angkor, as are pants or skirts that extend below the knees, and shirts that cover the shoulders. If you show up in a tank top or shorts, you'll be turned

away, but you needn't go all the way back to your hotel to change. Vendors outside the temples sell inexpensive t-shirts and lightweight pajama-style pants that are ideal for the extremely hot and sticky climate.

UNESCO added Angkor to its World Heritage Sites list in 1992, when just 113,183 people visited. Twelve years later, it was removed from the list of sites in danger, whereupon tourism numbers swelled. By 2019, more than 6 million people annually were wandering through Angkor's ancient architecture.

The dramatic increase in visitors poses a real danger to the site, not so much because of the millions of shoes wearing down sandstone, but because of the water visitors require during their stay. As the hospitality industry draws more and more water from underground reservoirs, the water table subsides, causing many of Angkor's structures to sink. The COVID-19 pandemic brought Cambodian tourism to a standstill, giving local officials an opportunity to re-evaluate ways of bringing back visitors while preserving the attractions.

Vietnam

Dive into a nation on tFe move.

In so many of Vietnam's major cities, something as simple as crossing the street can be an adventure, and not one for the timid. The relentless torrent of cars, trucks, motorcycles, and scooters—oh so many scooters—through the major arteries never comes to a stop; it just slips around obstacles like water flowing downstream. The only way across the road is to plunge into the chaos, make eye contact with any driver who might run you over, and don't stop until you reach the other side.

The traffic is a pretty good metaphor for modern-day Vietnam. As recently as the mid-1980s, it was one of the poorest countries in the world. Today, however, it is regarded as one of the greatest economic success stories of the 20th century. Much of the credit for this transformation belongs to the 1986 Doi Moi (rejuvenation) program, which dismantled the country's planned, agrarian economy, and opened the nation to international trade. Doi Moi also launched programs like rural electrification and universal primary school education, both of which have sustained Vietnam's progress well into the 21st century.

International tourism has also played a large part in this metamorphosis. And why not? The country is about three-quarters the size of California with

just as much variety. Vietnam's eight UNESCO World Heritage Sites include Hoi An (an exceptionally well-preserved example of a traditional Asian trading port) and Ha Long Bay, where traditional boats called junks sail through a gorgeous seascape of limestone karst pillars and thousands of unoccupied islands.

The Complex of Hue Monuments (also a World Heritage Site) preserves structures from the 19th century, when Hue was the political, cultural, and religious capital of the country. Hoa Lo Prison (nicknamed "Hanoi Hilton" by American POWs held there) focuses most of its attention not on the U.S. conflict but on the gruesome treatment that French jailers doled out to Vietnamese inmates.

For a deeper appreciation of the conflict known locally as "the American war," visit Ho Chi Minh City (formerly Saigon). The Museum of American War Crimes was renamed the War Remnants Museum in 1993, but it still paints a picture of the war heavily weighted on the local side. Another popular site is Reunification Palace, the home of South Vietnam's president until 1975, when North Vietnamese forces took it by force.

With so many other attractions competing for visitors' attention, Vietnam's beaches often get overlooked. That's a shame, as the country offers more than 1,865 miles (3,000 km) of coastline, much of it fronted by powdery sand beaches. Two of the best are adjacent to the cities of Nha Trang and Da Nang. While you're in Da Nang, don't miss the Golden Bridge, held aloft by a giant pair of hands.

Plan Your Trip

Location: Southeast Asia

Getting There: Both Hanoi and Ho Chi Minh City receive nonstop flights from Paris, London, and Istanbul, as well as dozens of Asian cities. Nonstop service from the U.S. is available from San Francisco to Ho Chi Minh City and between Anchorage and Hanoi.

When to Go: This depends on which part of the country you visit. In Hanoi and other parts of Northern Vietnam, the dry season (November-April) is prime time. But that's also when Ho Chi Minh City and Southern Vietnam get hot and muggy. September is probably the best overall month for traveling throughout the entire country. Hotel rates are usually highest during the celebration of Tet in January or February.

Bangkok

Savor it before it sinks.

If you're only going to visit one temple in Bangkok, you've probably come to the wrong place. The city is practically inundated with wats (the Thai word for temple), and many of them are worth a peek in entirely different ways. At Wat Arun, for example, visitors can climb the steep and narrow stairs to the top of the temple's 269-foot (82-meter) central tower, where they're rewarded with one of the best views in all of Thailand. Sunrise is the best time to visit, and not just because Wat Arun means "temple of the dawn"; daybreak is one of the few times this temple isn't crowded.

Wat Pho sits a short ferry ride across the Chao Phraya River and is as horizontal as Wat Arun is vertical. It's renowned for a 151-foot (50-meter) gold-plated reclining Buddha statue, which takes up almost the entire building. An additional 393 Buddhas are tucked in nooks and crannies throughout the temple's four chapels. A block away is the Temple of the Emerald Buddha, one of the highlights of the Grand Palace, which was Thailand's royal residence until 1925. This Buddha was carved

in the 15th century, and the temple is considered the most sacred in all of Thailand. Be sure to wear clothing that covers your shoulders and knees when visiting temples.

Plan Your Trip

Location: Thailand

Getting There: There are no nonstop flights to Bangkok from North America, but there are from Europe's major capitals as well as from dozens of cities in Asia, Africa, the Middle East, and both Sidney and Melbourne.

When to Go: Avoid Thailand's monsoon season (May-October). Prices are cheaper during this period, but you'll pay in other ways. From November to April, the temperature is cooler and rain showers are infrequent. Every April, the city celebrates the Buddhist New Year with Songkran, a festival in which people throw or shoot water at each other as part of a cleansing ritual.

If all this sightseeing makes you hungry, you're definitely in the right place, as countless Bangkok attractions revolve around eating. The city's street food scene, especially in Chinatown (Yaowarat), is unrivaled, and many items cost no more than $3. On weekends, fresh fruit and vegetables arrive by canoe at the floating markets at Khlong Lad Myon and Taling Chan. Perhaps the best floating market, however, is Damnoen Saduak. foodie visitors put in a little extra effort to travel there, since it's an hour outside of the city.

Getting out on the water is a terrific way to tour Bangkok, which earned the nickname "the Venice of the East" for its vast network of waterways and canals known as klongs. Hire a longtail boat to shepherd you through hidden backwaters; book a table for two on a dinner cruise of the Chao Phraya River; or ride the public ferries and water taxis from one attraction to another.

Like many low-lying cities in Southeast Asia, Bangkok is vulnerable to flooding, as evidenced by the 2011 deluge that killed 815 people and caused more than $46 billion worth of damage. But that's only half the story. Thailand's capital is built on highly compactable layers of soft clay, which are subsiding by half an inch (1.25 cm) per year. The World Bank predicts that 70% of flood costs will be due to land subsidence rather than sea level rise. Some experts predict the entire city could be underwater by 2040.

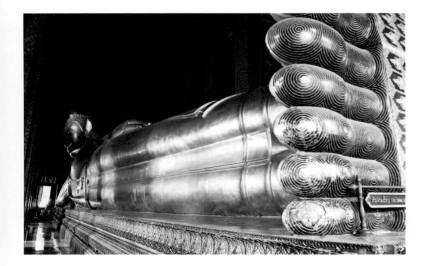

Borneo

Hang with orangutans in the world's oldest rain forest.

The very mention of the word Borneo conjures up images of an imaginary paradise lost to history centuries ago, like Plato's allegorical Atlantis. Most people can't place the island on a map, but they know it's someplace exotic. In truth, Borneo is very much a real place, an Eden-like jungle barely touched by the forces of time.

But conservationists fear that activities like logging, poaching, mining, and farming could pose an existential threat to Borneo's flora and fauna, especially its population of critically endangered orangutans. Nicknamed "the old men of the jungle," these primates are one of humankind's closest relatives, sharing 96.4% of our DNA. But they reproduce only once every three to five years, making it hard for them to recover from population declines.

Plan Your Trip

Location: Southeast Asia. Borneo, the world's third-largest island, is divided among three nations: Malaysia, Indonesia, and Brunei.

Getting There: Located in the northeastern corner of Malaysian Borneo, Kota Kinabalu International Airport is the largest airport on the island; it receives nonstop flights from Singapore, Kuala Lumpur, Bangkok, Taiwan, Hong Kong, Manila, Tokyo, and Seoul. Indonesian Borneo has two smaller international airports, and Brunei has one.

When to Go: The dry season (April-October) is the best time to visit. The heavy rains during monsoon season (November-March) typically cool down Borneo's tropical heat but play havoc with schedules for flights and riverboat adventures.

Deforestation is perhaps the biggest threat to the orangutan's survival. Cutting down trees to build palm oil plantations destroys vital habitat for the slow-moving animals, forcing them to range farther for food and come into conflict with people. As much as half of Borneo's rain forests have been demolished in recent years; and as demand for palm oil continues to soar, that trend is likely to continue.

Borneo's orangutan population numbers just over 100,000, which makes it seem like the odds of seeing them are pretty good. But Borneo is the size of Texas, and most of the orangutans prefer to stay in the less developed parts of the island. Approximately 500 orangutans have been known to hang out in the Danum Valley, part of a 150-square-mile (389-sq.-km) rain forest reserve in Borneo's northeast corner. Orangutan sightings are less common at the 300,000-acre (121,405-hectare) Tabin Wildlife Reserve, also in northeast Malaysian Borneo, but pygmy elephants, Sumatran Rhinos, and more than 300 bird species are found within its confines.

The Kinabatangan Wildlife Sanctuary is another excellent location for a photo safari, and a river (the Kinabatangan) runs through it, making it ideal for exploring by boat. There are almost no trails in this dense jungle, so bring binoculars that will allow you to see without getting out of the boat. In addition to wild orangutans, you may spot pygmy elephants, monitor lizards, crocodiles, and eight different species of hornbills

For near-guaranteed orangutan sightings, stop in at Sepilok Orangutan Rehabilitation Centre, which provides care for orphan orangutans, as well as the occasional gibbon, elephant, or sun bear (a small ursine species found only in southeast Asia). Because baby orangutans stay with their mothers for six years, rehabilitation can be a long process. The most important skill orphans need to survive in the wild is climbing, something they learn from older animals. The center is open 365 days a year; feeding times are 10 AM and 3 PM.

Borobudur Temple

Seek nirvana at the world's largest Buddhist monument.

The world's largest Buddhist temple is truly a spectacle. Its central structure is a 95-foot (29-meter) step pyramid, erected more than 1,200 years ago from two million stones carried from local rivers and pieced together without mortar. Nearly 3,000 bas-relief sculptures depicting the life and teachings of the Buddha adorn the temple's lower square terraces, and its circular upper levels feature dozens of stone-lattice stupas, many of them with a statue of Buddha in the center. For the devout, climbing the temple's multiple levels was (and is) a pilgrimage to ever-higher levels of consciousness on their journey to enlightenment.

Sometime between the 10th and 15th centuries (when Islam became the dominant religion in Indonesia), the temple was abandoned, buried beneath volcanic ash, and reclaimed by the jungle. Thomas Raffles, the British governor of Java, had the site uncovered in the early 19th century, which revealed its treasures to the wider world, but also exposed them to the elements. A restoration project in 1907-1911 stabilized the temple walls and improved its drainage system. An even more ambitious effort from the late 1960s to the 1980s (with UNESCO's help) dismantled, cleaned, and

Plan Your Trip

Location: Kedu Valley near Yogyakarta, Central Java, Indonesia

Getting There: Yogyakarta International Airport, completed in 2020, receives daily flights from most of Indonesia's largest cities. A planned expansion should receive international flights. Borobudur is about a 90-minute drive from the airport, or an hour from the city of Yogyakarta.

When to Go: Indonesia is tropical year-round. July through September are ideal months to visit, with the lowest temperatures and the least precipitation.

rebuilt the relief walls and galleries. More than a million stones were removed, treated against weathering, and reassembled.

UNESCO added the Borobudur temple compound (including the smaller Mendut and Pawon temples, which form a straight line directly east of the main temple) to its World Heritage Site list in 1991. Like Borobudur itself, the three monuments also represent phases in the attainment of nirvana.

Today's visitors may experience Borobudur the same way ninth-century pilgrims did when the temple was first built, climbing their own path to enlightenment, and perhaps stopping along the way to admire the views of Mt. Merapi. This volcano erupted most recently in 2010, coating the temple in acidic ash (since removed). Locals often refer to the fertile agricultural region surrounding the temple complex as "the garden of Java." Hiring a local guide is an inexpensive way to learn about the significance of the statues and sculptures as you encounter them. Sunrise and sunset are said to be magical times to visit.

A 2006 earthquake in Yogyakarta that killed more than 5,000 people spared the temple, but Borobudur might not be so lucky in future tremors. The experts at the Borobudur Heritage Conservation Institute also worry about another volcanic eruption and about acid rain, which has already eroded many of the 1,200-year-old bas-reliefs.

Ujung Kulon National Park

Catch a glimpse of the world's last Javan rhinos.

The Javan rhino is the most endangered of the five rhinoceros species—the Sumatran rhino is a disturbingly close second—and one of the most critically endangered animals on the planet. Only 75 of the one-horned animals are known to survive anywhere on earth, all of them in Indonesia's Ujung Kulon National Park, located on a peninsula at the southwest end of the island of Java. (Ujung Kulon means western end in Indonesian.)

Javan rhinos once roamed widely throughout Southeast Asia, but hunting and habitat loss drove their numbers down to just a handful by the end of the twentieth century. While not a complete success

story yet, organized efforts to protect the remaining population have prevented further loss of animals, and at least one new calf has been born every year since 2012, according to Save the Rhino Trust. Ujung Kulon has been a UNESCO World Heritage Site since 1991, and a rhino hasn't been poached here in more than 20 years.

Despite the gains of the last decade, the Javan rhino still faces a number of threats. The park's 194,272 acres (78,619 hectares) can't support many more rhinos, and the invasive Arenga palm is blocking sunlight from the plants that rhinos like to eat. The park's location near the volcanic

Rhinos aren't the only reason to visit Ujung Kulon; indeed, sightings are so rare that some locals regard the rhino as a mythical creature. But the park is home to 29 other mammal species, including leopards, wild dogs, Javan mongoose, and three endemic primate species: Javan gibbons, Javan red leaf monkeys, and silvered leaf monkeys. Despite the park's relative proximity to Jakarta, it receives relatively few visitors. Most people visit as part of an organized tour, as there are no roads within the park.

island of Krakatoa (site of the storied 1883 volcanic eruption that killed 36,000 people) makes it vulnerable to tsunamis. The Javan Rhino Study and Conservation Area has cleared Arenga palms from an additional 12,355 acres (5 000 hectares) of rhino habitat on the park's eastern end and is actively looking for locations beyond Java to establish new rhino populations.

Plan Your Trip

Location: Banten province, Java, Indonesia

Getting There: The park is about a six-hour drive from Jakarta, the capital, over roads that aren't terribly well-maintained. It is also possible to arrive by a three-hour boat ride from Carita Beach. Cities with nonstop flights to Jakarta include Amsterdam, Istanbul, Sydney, Tokyo, Seoul, and Bangkok.

When to Go: Rhinos and other wildlife are easiest to see during the dry season (April-October). There are relatively few accommodations within the park other than primitive campgrounds, so plan ahead.

Komodo National Park

See dragons, preferably before they see you.

In early 2019, Indonesian officials announced they were closing Komodo National Park to tourism for up to a year because too many visitors were stealing the park's namesake dragons and selling the endangered species on the black market. Less than six months later, the environment and forestry ministry reversed the decision but suggested the country could combat poaching instead by raising the entry fee to a whopping $1,000.

Then coronavirus intervened, curbing international travel, and accomplishing much the same ends as the proposed tourism ban. But the episode was emblematic of Indonesia's contradictory approach to protecting the world's largest lizard. The park has an active management plan and an agency to monitor incursions. But at the same time, Indonesia has encouraged wholesale increases in tourism to the area. In 2015, the country added a new terminal to the airport in the nearby city of Labuan Bajo, renaming it Komodo Airport, and increasing its annual capacity tenfold to 1.5 million passengers.

The name change makes it safe to assume that many of those additional visitors will go in search of Komodo dragons, which exist only on the large

Plan Your Trip

Location: Lesser Sunda Islands, Indonesia

Getting There: Komodo Airport is located on Flores, the largest island in the region. It receives flights from Jakarta, Denpasar, Surabaya, Ende, and Kupang. Most visitors explore the park by boat.

When to Go: The dry season (April-November) is the best time to visit, although this is also the hottest time of year. Expect light rain in December and March. Avoid monsoon season (January-February).

island of Flores and four smaller islands off its west coast. And for good reason: Komodo dragons are kind of an evolutionary missing link. They grow up to 10 feet (3 meters) long, weigh up to 330 pounds (149 kg), have no predators, and can run as fast as a person. Their venomous bite prevents blood from clotting, causing their prey to bleed to death. Dragons can kill animals as big as a water buffalo and can eat up to 80% of their body weight in a single feeding. Dragons don't often attack humans, but they have.

There are fewer than 6,000 Komodo dragons left on earth, with the greatest concentration found on Komodo, one of the three main volcanic islands that make up Komodo National Park. The best way to experience the park is on a boat tour from Labuan Bajo. Accompanied by a park ranger, visitors can walk the trails that crisscross the island in hopes of seeing one of these rare animals. The surrounding reefs are rich with marine biodiversity, including dolphins, whales, dugongs, turtles, massive manta rays, and thousands of other fish species. One of the most popular spots—for snorkelers, scuba divers, and landlubbers alike—is Pantai Merah, also known as Pink Beach.

A UNESCO World Heritage site since 1991, the park is vulnerable

in myriad ways. Overfishing and litter threaten underwater species, while a sponge known as *Chalienula nematifera* is killing coral. Increasing tourism numbers and a growing local population both pose risks in encroachment on habitat for dragons and other wildlife. Potential effects of climate change include more fires in the forests and coral bleaching caused by warmer seas.

Shanghai

Visit the "City on the Sea" before it becomes the "City in the Sea."

China's largest city is also one of its most vibrant: a prosperous, fast-moving metropolis whose iconic skyline seems to be adding a new landmark every day. Shanghai was once known as the Paris of the Orient. The better comparison, however, might be New York, another commercial and financial waterfront city that never sleeps. There's always something happening at the world's busiest port.

Shanghai literally means "City on the Sea" in Chinese, and there's no better place to start exploring than the waterfront promenade known as the Bund. Located in the older Puxi half of the city, the Bund was Shanghai's original center of commerce, a wide boulevard where rice was traded, powerful banks occupied stately neoclassical and art deco buildings, and fortunes were won and lost. Nanjing Road,

Shanghai's answer to Beverly Hills's Rodeo Drive, starts at the Bund and continues six miles west, lined by luxury boutiques and department stores. From the Bund, walking west along Nanjing Road for a little over a mile (1.6 km) brings you to the Shanghai Museum, repository of more than a million artifacts from China's history and an architectural jewel itself. Admission is free, but go early.

The other reason people make the Bund their first stop is to look across the Huangpu River at the ever-taller skyscrapers rising from Shanghai's newer Pudong side. Any time is a good time to stroll here, but the views are best at night when the buildings are lit up (and the smog doesn't hamper visibility). Shanghai Tower is the tallest building in the skyline and third-highest in the world, but the most recognizable landmark is the iconic Oriental Pearl TV Tower, whose orbs were erected in 1991 and still look futuristic more than 30 years later.

For a more calming experience (but no less crowded, especially during Chinese New Year), stop in at the Jade Buddha Temple, whose centerpiece is a reclining Buddha statue carved from a single piece of white jade. Built in 1918-1928, the temple remains one of Shanghai's few active Buddhist monasteries.

Shanghai isn't the city most at risk from sea-level rise, but it is the largest. Nearly 35 million people live in the urban area, more than half of them on land that likely will be underwater if global temperatures continue to climb at current rates. China has been preparing for this worst-case scenario by building hundreds of miles of protective seawalls all along Hangzhou Bay and encircling the islands of Chongming, Hengsha, and Changzing.

Plan Your Trip

Location: Southeastern China

Getting There: Pudong International Airport is one of the world's largest; it receives flights from five continents. Hongqiao International Airport is smaller, with flights arriving mostly from China and other nearby Asian countries. To get to downtown from Pudong, hop on a Shanghai MagLev train, which hurtles passengers at 270 miles per hour (434 km/h).

When to Go: The weather here is also a lot like New York: cold in winter and hot in summer. Spring (April-May) and fall (October-November) are ideal times to visit; hotel rates are usually lower than in the peak summer season (June-September). Because Shanghai is a business-first city, hotel rates are often lower on weekends.

Forbidden City

You can see clearly now, the smog has gone.

The world's largest imperial palace is forbidden in name only. Home to emperors for half a millennium, China's single-most-popular attraction has been open to the public since 1925 and now draws more than 15 million visitors annually.

The Forbidden City is officially named The Palace Museum, but that doesn't begin to describe this massive campus of parade grounds, ramparts, courtyards, and museum galleries, surrounded by a 171-foot (52-meter) moat. UNESCO, which declared the city a World Heritage Site in 1987, identifies it as the world's largest collection of preserved ancient wooden structures. The complex is about the same size as Disneyland, but with fewer trees and less shade, so you'll want to wear good walking shoes and plenty of sunscreen.

All visitors enter the Forbidden City through the Meridian Gate adjacent to Tiananmen Square. A guided tour will help you make sense of the thousands of things to see—including the hundreds of cats, some descended from felines kept by Ming dynasty concubines. If you prefer to explore independently, be sure to buy an official map from one of the shops just inside the Meridian Gate.

The most popular tour takes about two hours and hits the highlights along the city's central axis: the Hall of Supreme Harmony, the Hall of Middle Harmony,

the Hall of Preserving Harmony, the Palace of Heavenly Purity (the emperor's bedroom), and a few other must-see buildings, before ending at the Imperial Garden. For a less crowded experience, venture off to the left or right to less-visited gems like the Hall of Mental Cultivation, the Pavilion of Literary Profundity (the Royal Library), the Hall of Abstinence, or the Treasure Gallery in the Palace of Tranquil Longevity.

Jingshan Park sits across the street from the Gate of Spiritual Valor at the north end, where all visitors exit the Forbidden City. Be sure to walk the short trail up to Wanchun Pavilion for an elevated bird's-eye view of the Forbidden City.

For many years, the city (indeed all of Beijing) was off the tourist circuit because of smog so thick it was hazardous just to be outside. In 2013, the city suffered through a so-called "air-pocalypse," when concentrations of noxious particulate matter reached levels 90 times higher than what the World Health Organization deemed safe to breathe. That was also the same year President Xi Jinping declared war against air pollution, banning construction of new coal-fired power plants. In 2021, the capital recorded its lowest level of emissions since 2013, and "Beijing blue" skies were commonplace, but the ban expired in 2018.

Plan Your Trip

Location: Beijing, China

Getting There: Beijing Capital International Airport receives direct flights from a half-dozen North American cities. The complex is easily accessible by subway, bus, or taxi.

When to Go: April, May, October, and November are ideal months. The weather is temperate and there are fewer crowds than during peak summer season (June-September).

Great Wall of China

Visit a sprawling ancient architectural wonder.

A UNESCO World Heritage site since 1987, China's Great Wall is actually a network of fortifications, built over 2,000 years. People think of it as a single structure because the section closest to Beijing extends for nearly 1,400 miles (2,250 km), from the Gobi Desert to the Yellow Sea. This segment is known as the Ming Wall because it was erected during that dynasty (1368-1644 CE).

Unlike some sections built from earth and straw, most of the Ming Wall sits on a solid foundation of bricks and stones held together with mortar made from lime and—believe it or not—sticky rice. The bond is so tight that weeds don't even grow through it and so sturdy that it has helped the Wall survive thousands of earthquakes.

Tour buses line up outside the Badaling Scenic Area, located about an hour's drive northwest of Beijing. More than 10 million people annually

flooded this section before the Chinese government limited the daily visitor number to 65,000 in 2019. Equally popular is Mutianyu (about 90 minutes from the capital by car), where a cable car, chair lift, and toboggan ride make the impeccably restored section of wall easily accessible.

For a less crowded experience, visit a section that hasn't been fully restored. In partially renovated sections like Huanghuacheng or Jianshanling, you'll get to see something besides the back of the visitor walking directly in front of you. Huanghuacheng (90 minutes from Beijing) traces the south shore of Haoming Lake, crosses the lake atop a dam, and is completely submerged under the water in places. Its often-steep steps aren't in mint condition, but they're still safe to climb. Or you can take a boat trip on the lake to see the wall from afar.

The drive to Jianshanling is about two hours, but well worth it for its unfettered access to 67 watchtowers (about one every 500 feet/150 meters). There's even a cable car to ferry visitors from the ticket gate up to Little Jinshan Tower.

After two millennia, it shouldn't be surprising that parts of the wall are crumbling. By some estimates, fully half of the original wall has been lost to erosion and other natural forces. In other areas, portions are impassable because, during the 1970s, some officials encouraged residents to remove bricks and stones from the wall for other construction. (Such looting is now illegal.)

Plan Your Trip

Location: The UNESCO-protected section of the Great Wall begins in the east at Shanhaiguan in Hebei province and ends at Jiayuguan in Gansu province to the west.

Getting There: Badaling or Mutianyu can both be accessed via public transportation from Beijing, but many visitors hire a private car or visit as part of an organized tour.

When to Go: Fall (September-November) has mild weather and a fraction of the visitors who crowd the sections closest to Beijing during the peak summer season.

Yangtze River

Take a slow boat through China.

For travelers daunted by getting around in a massive country without much English signage, a Yangtze River cruise might be just the ticket. Once you board the ship, you're surrounded only by fellow passengers, and the scenery comes to you. Yangtze River cruises cater to guests at every budget and level of comfort, from bunk beds and squat toilets to luxury cabins and impressive cuisine.

The best Yangtze River cruises start in Chongqing and end three or four days later downstream in Yichang. For many passengers, the highlight of a Yangtze River cruise comes at the end, as you float through the complex locks adjacent to the monumental Three Gorges Dam. The vision of China's first president, Sun-Yat Sen back in 1919, the world's largest hydropower plant came to fruition in 2003. In addition to providing electricity for millions of residents in the Yangtze River Valley, the multibillion-dollar project is expected to control the kind of devastating flooding that plagued the region in the past.

More than 1,000 towns were submerged to complete the project, requiring the relocation of over a million people. You can usually see evidence of this upheaval at Fengdu, where most cruises stop on the first day. The city was rebuilt higher up the mountainside, as the original location is now underwater. The new city is on the opposite side of the river from a popular attraction known as Fengdu Ghost City, a complex of Han Dynasty temples and shrines dedicated to the afterlife. Visitors complete a series of mental and physical challenges before being allowed to advance to the next milestone.

What you won't see in your cruise line's promotional materials, however, is the challenge pollution poses on the Yangtze River. In addition to carrying cruise ship passengers, China's longest river is a major commercial artery, with cargo vessels discharging in both the air and the water. Businesses, factories, and residents along the banks of the river also produce waste. With help from the World Bank, China launched a multibillion-dollar project to clean up the river basin in 2021. Whether it is too little too late remains to be seen.

Plan Your Trip

Location: The Yangtze flows east from the Tanggula Mountains for 3,900 miles (6,300 km) to the China Sea near Shanghai.

Getting There: The best cruises depart from Chongqing, whose Jiangbei International Airport receives flights from Singapore, Bangkok, Sydney, Tokyo, and dozens of Chinese cities.

When to Go: Most cruises operate from April to October. Spring (April-May) and fall (September-October) have the best weather and smaller crowds than the height of summer.

Sakura Season

Walk through cherry blossoms for a reminder of life's impermanence.

Cherry blossoms are serious business in Japan. The rite of spring is so treasured that Japan's national meteorological office puts out an annual forecast of where and when the blooms will peak in different parts of the country. Sakura (Japanese for "cherry tree") season usually kicks off in subtropical Okinawa in late January and continues through early May, when the northernmost reaches of Hokkaido join in the festivities. In most of the places visited by international travelers, however, blooms usually peak around April.

Entire festivals have built up around hanami ("flower viewing"), many of which involve picnics, barbecues, live music, craft fairs, or tea ceremonies underneath the pink boughs. In some locations, lights or paper lanterns are hung from the trees for night viewing known in Japanese as yazakura, in which sake might enliven the goings-on.

Tokyo's Shinjuku Gyoen has some of the country's best viewing, with more than 1,000 trees, including many that bloom early and others that bloom late, extending blossom season to nearly a

Plan Your Trip

Location: Throughout Japan

Getting There: Tokyo International Airport (a.k.a. Haneda) and Narita International Airport are among the world's busiest, receiving nonstop flights from dozens of countries worldwide. Osaka, Kansai, and Nagoya also have international airports.

When to Go: Spring. Visit the Japan Weather Association's website (www.jwa.or.jp) for detailed forecasts of when blooms will peak.

solid month. Nearly 5,000 sakura line the banks of Osaka's Okawa River, making a river cruise a novel way to experience the season. The greatest concentration is on Mount Yoshino, which has been carpeted in 30,000 cherry trees since the 8th century. Takato Castle Park in Nagano has one of the livelier festivals, and excellent nighttime illuminations. For a more meditative experience,

stroll Kyoto's Philosopher's Path, where a 1.5-mile (2-km) walkway parallels a canal lined with hundreds of cherry trees.

In 2021, Kyoto's sakura reached their peak bloom on March 26, the earliest date since the country started collecting official data in 1953. Researchers at Osaka University said it was the earliest peak bloom in more than 1,200 years, based on historical diaries from emperors, aristocrats, and monks. Scientists attribute the earlier blooms to climate change.

An even more disturbing bloom came to several parts of Japan in October 2018, six months ahead of schedule. Scientists believe that premature explosion was due to typhoon Jebi, which blew the leaves off the trees in September, followed by warm weather that persuaded the trees it was spring again. In years to come, visitors planning cherry blossom-viewing trips to Japan may have to wait until the last minute to figure out where and when to go.

Mount Fuji

Japan's tallest summit isn't as high as it seems.

Japan's tallest mountain hovers over the Tokyo horizon, luring visitors to its snow-capped slopes less than three hours from Tokyo. Up close, however, the mountain looks quite different than it does from afar. The summit is just 12,388 feet (3,776 meters) and you can drive halfway to the top. There are bathrooms (bring coins), convenience stands, and warming huts along the way, and even Wi-Fi at the top.

All of these things combine to make Mount Fuji one of the world's most popular hikes. It's a hike, not a climb, because unless there's snow at the top, you don't need any mountaineering equipment besides warm clothing and a good pair of hiking shoes. Fit hikers can finish the easiest route in half a day, but because sunrise has been ballyhooed as

the time to see the view from the top, thousands of people stop for the night at a hostel near the summit and rise a few hours before dawn the next day. (Add a flashlight or headlamp to your pack if you do.) This schedule has the added benefit of acclimating visitors to the altitude.

UNESCO declared Mt. Fuji a World Heritage Site in 2013 for its cultural value, not its natural beauty. Surprisingly, though, the inscription hasn't affected visitation that much. The weather has more of an impact on how many people make it to the top: around 200,000 over a cold summer and perhaps twice as many if the snow melts early. For some visitors, sharing the mountain with 3,000 other hikers per day makes for camaraderie. For others, the long line of people trudging their

way up the slopes isn't exactly an escape to the great outdoors.

Graffiti, trash, and human waste are among the problems that accompany any site visited by so many people. There's also concern that Mt. Fuji is still technically an active stratovolcano, although it hasn't erupted since 1707. The greater worry, however, is climate change. In 2021, scientists found that the tree line, the boundary above which trees cannot grow, had risen about 100 feet (30 meters) up the slope since 1978, with most of the increase coming in the last two decades. The average maximum temperature at the summit, meanwhile, has increased about 4°F (2°C) over the past 50 years.

Plan Your Trip

Location: Yamanashi and Shizuoka prefectures, Honshu island, Japan

Getting There: The mountain is less than three hours by car from Tokyo. There is also frequent bus and train service from the capital to the Fujiyoshida, Gotemba, and Fujinomiya stations.

When to Go: The best time to climb is summer (early July-September). Spring and fall can be as bitingly cold as winter, so carry winter gear or avoid the climb outside of the summer season. Mountain Day, usually August 11, is one of the most crowded times.

AUSTRALIA, OCEANIA, AND ANTARCTICA

Great Barrier Reef

Take in astonishing sites above and below the water's surface

The world's largest coral reef system is roughly the size of Japan, so big, in fact, that it's the only living organism that can be seen from outer space with the naked eye. Its immense 1,400-mile (2,253-km) range provides a habitat for 1,500 species of tropical fish, 30 species of whales and dolphins, the world's largest clams, and six of the world's seven species of turtles. Opportunities for swimming alongside these majestic sea creatures abound throughout the reef.

Australia's underwater equivalent of Africa's Big Five safari animals is known as the Great Eight, an octet of species that every Reef visitor hopes to see while on holiday. In addition to turtles, whales, and giant clams, the Great Eight includes manta rays,

clownfish (the colorful starring species of *Finding Nemo*), hundreds of species of sharks (almost all of them harmless to humans), and the potato cod and the Maori wrasse, two fish species that can grow to more than six feet in length.

The scenery above the water isn't too shabby either. The 85-mile (138-km) drive on the mainland from Cairns to Cape Tribulation rivals California's Pacific Coast Highway for gorgeous coastal scenery (with a fraction of the traffic). But the real beauty of this region lies in the islands floating just offshore—more than 900 of them in total. Lizard Island is equally popular with reptiles and Hollywood celebrities looking to escape the spotlight. On

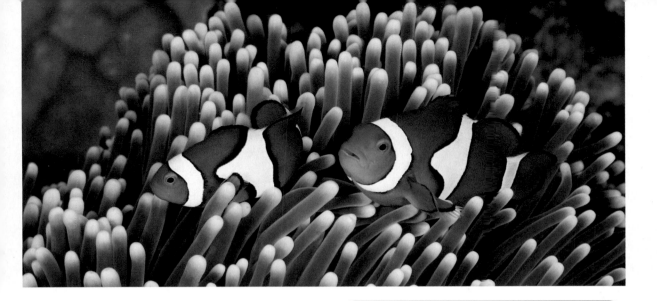

Magnetic Island, the vibe is even more chill—a state that agrees with the large population of resident koalas. Many travelers island-hop from one sugary-white sand beach to another in the Whitsundays archipelago, where hiking trails and rain forests also abound.

The reef has been a UNESCO World Heritage Site since 1981, but that hasn't completely shielded it from environmental degradation. Over the past 20 years, rising ocean temperatures around the reef have spawned multiple episodes of coral bleaching, causing the brilliantly colored organisms to lose their awe-inspiring hues. In some cases, bleaching events kill the coral completely. Some scientists estimate the reef could be completely extinct as soon as 2050.

Plan Your Trip

Location: Queensland, Australia

Getting There: Cairns Airport is the gateway to most destinations on the reef, but some of the southernmost islands can be accessed directly from Brisbane Airport, which has more direct international flights from Asia and the U.S. west coast.

When to Go: June thru October is the dry season, which makes for the best snorkeling and diving visibility. The rainy season (November-March) can also be muggy with humidity. The shoulder season from April to May carries the risk of occasional rain showers, but also pleasant temperatures in the low 80s and lower prices than in the dry season.

Blue Mountains

Seven national parks showcase the beauty in Sydney's backyard.

Ninety minutes west of Sydney lie Australia's Blue Mountains, a landscape thoroughly unlike Uluru, the Reef, or any of the major cities down under. Prescient early explorers of the Great Dividing Range recognized its natural beauty and endeavored to preserve it. Even the towns peppered throughout the forest have retained old world charm. A UNESCO World Heritage site since 2000, the Greater Blue Mountains Area encompasses seven different national parks, plus the Jenolan Caves Karst Conservation Reserve (the world's oldest cave system, at 340 million years of age).

The highest point in the Blue Mountains is just 3,901 feet (1,189 meters) and doesn't even have a formal name. That's because many of its faces are too steep to hike. The most popular trails don't ascend the mountains; they traverse the range horizontally from one magnificent vista to another. A major exception is Giant Stairway, a series of 988 steep steps carved into the side of the mountains. It's not for the faint of heart.

By contrast, almost everybody can travel the half-mile (0.8-km) wheelchair-accessible trail to Echo Point and snap selfies in front of Three Sisters formation, which looks especially impressive at sunset. Other popular viewpoints include Pulpit Rock and Govetts Leap Lookout.

At the privately run Scenic World, it's even easier to get around. The glass-walled Scenic Skyway gondola carries visitors horizontally across a 1,000-foot (305-meter) chasm. The Scenic Railway is the world's steepest incline train, ascending nearly 1,000 feet (305 meters) at a 52-degree angle. The Scenic Skyway cable car whisks sightseers 1,500 feet (457 meters) from top to bottom in just 8 minutes.

Fire has been a natural part of the Blue Mountain ecosystem's life cycle for as long as humans have inhabited the continent. But the infernos of the 21st century are a different story altogether. These fires burn hotter, longer, and more frequently than the fires of the previous 60,000 years, giving biodiversity fewer opportunities to regenerate. The conflagration that ravaged the Blueys in 2019-20 was the largest fire in New South Wales history. It burned for three months, incinerating more than two million acres of forest, along with habitat for an estimated 140 million

animals. As the planet warms and drought becomes more persistent, blazes of this size and duration may soon become the norm.

Plan Your Trip

Location: New South Wales, Australia

Getting There: The Blue Mountains are about a 90-minute drive from Sydney, Australia's largest city. You can rent a car, or you can hop on the Blue Mountains train from Sydney's Central station and ride a trolley bus from hotels to most of the major attractions.

When to Go: There's no bad time to visit the Blue Mountains. Spring (September to November) has the best weather—temperatures in the 70s °F (low 20s °C) and little rain, so it's the most popular time of year to visit. Autumn (March to May) is not quite as busy but popular with visitors in search of fall color. Winter (June-August) can bring snow, a plus for anyone who'd like to see the landscape with a light white dusting. Summer (December to February) is warm, sometimes uncomfortably so, but usually cooler than Sydney, so it's a popular escape from the city, especially around the holidays.

12 Apostles of the Great Ocean Road

Land and water meet spectacularly on one of the world's great drives.

Just so there's no confusion, there were never 12 Apostles in Victoria. The Englishman who first encountered the impressive limestone stacks here called them Sow and Piglets; Victoria tourism officials coined the moniker The Apostles to bring visitors, who ultimately gave it the numbered misnomer, even though only nine of them ever stood here. Since a 2005 collapse, there have been eight.

The same erosive forces that created these figures is expected to reduce (or possibly increase) the number in years to come. Additional stacks may separate from the mainland, while others may tumble into the sea. In 1990, for example, the formation nicknamed London Bridge because of its two spans over the water got a quick rebranding as London Arch when one of the spans collapsed.

The Apostles are perhaps the best-known feature of the Great Ocean Road, a 150-mile (241-km) ribbon of blacktop along Victoria's southern coastline. The route starts in Torquay, about an hour southwest of Melbourne, and ends in Allansford, near Warrnambool, the largest city along

Plan Your Trip

Location: Victoria, Australia

Getting There: Melbourne is the closest international airport to the eastern end of the route in Torquay, about an hour away. After reaching Allansford, some visitors continue driving along the southern coast all the way to Adelaide, in South Australia. That adds about seven hours of driving to the journey.

When to Go: Australian summer (December-February) is the most popular and crowded season for driving the Great Ocean Road. Spring wildflowers line the route from September-November. The water is still warm enough for swimming in March and early April. Southern Right Whales return to Warrnambool to calve between June and September.

the route. In theory, you could drive the whole route and back in one day, but you wouldn't see much beyond the view from your windshield.

More to the point, the Apostles are just one of dozens of attractions along the way. Beelining it straight to them would be to miss out on seeing koalas along the Kennet River, strolling through a forest to the 100-foot (30-meter) Hopetoun Falls, soaking in natural hot springs, paddling with platypi in Great Otway National Park, or enjoying a picnic lunch on any of the hundreds of stretches of sand along the way. Childers Cove, meanwhile, 30 miles (48 km) beyond the Apostles, boasts similar limestone stacks, without all the crowds.

The greatest threat to the Great Ocean Road isn't climate change; it's unsustainable tourism. Too many visitors arrive on giant buses that stop in the same places at the same time. They strain 100-year-old roads and create traffic jams at the junctions where parking is tight. Recognizing the importance of preserving its most iconic road trip, Victoria's government passed the Great Ocean Road and Environs Protection Act of 2020, establishing a single agency to oversee the entire route.

Kakadu National Park

Experience a part of Australia that has barely changed in 40,000 years.

Australia's largest national park is a hard place for most visitors to access, but it's well worth the extra effort. Aboriginal peoples have lived in this remote part of Australia for more than 40,000 years, but a variety of deterrents have long kept outsiders away. Most of the sites in the park require a four-wheel drive vehicle to explore properly. And a fierce monsoon season (December–March) floods the lowland hills and woodlands, brings heat and stifling humidity to the coastal mangrove forests, and makes getting around even more challenging.

Kakadu is *Crocodile Dundee* territory—indeed, many of the 1986 film's scenes were shot in the park, including one at the swimming hole below Gunlom Falls, which is thankfully crocodile-free. For a glimpse of reptiles from a safe distance, and some first-hand insight into the Indigenous people who call this region home, hop on a Guluyambi Cultural Cruise, run by local Aboriginal guides.

Birds are the main animal attraction in Kakadu. One-third of all Australia's bird species (more than 300 in all) are found throughout the park's

the Bowali Visitor Centre and at the Marrawuddi Arts and Culture Centre.

Fire is a constant worry everywhere in Australian bush country, and saltwater intrusion into Kakadu's freshwater rivers and lakes is increasingly of concern. Another major threat is invasive animal species. Cane toads, pigs, and feral cats in particular have caused severe declines in some of Kakadu's native fauna.

7,000 square miles. From the observation platform in the Mamukala wetlands you may spot kites, cormorants, kingfishers, and purple swamp hens.

The Burrungkuy (Nourlangie) region is where you'll find a short walking trail through countless rock art paintings. A short but steep walk brings you to Nawurlandja lookout, a favored sunset spot. More recent examples of Aboriginal art—and sometimes the artists themselves—are on hand at

Plan Your Trip

Location: Northern Territory, Australia

Getting There: Darwin is the closest international airport to the park. From there it's about a three-hour drive to Jabiru, Kakadu's commercial center.

When to Go: Kakadu is hot year-round: hot and humid from December to March, and hot and dry from August-October. July and August are the driest months, but also the most crowded. May through early June is the Goldilocks window for most visitors: just the right combination of cool and dry weather before the waterfalls and swimming holes dry up for the season.

Fox and Franz Josef Glaciers

Trek across some of the world's most accessible glaciers.

New Zealand's Southern Alps are among the easiest places in the world to see glaciers. The Fox Glacier, for example, can be viewed just a short walk from the village of the same name. The neighboring Franz Josef Glacier (named by a European explorer in honor of the Austro-Hungarian emperor) sits amid an alpine playground chockablock with recreational activities that don't require ice axes.

New Zealand is home to more than 3,000 glaciers; what makes these two special is how close they are to the ocean. Both descend precipitously through temperate rain forest all the way to the Tasman Sea. This steepness accounts for glacial rivers that flow as much as 10 times as fast as those draining from other glaciers. And it makes for abrupt—and beautiful—changes of scene along the way.

This is a landscape of fjords, towering cliffs, majestic waterfalls, and serene alpine lakes like Lake Matheson, whose mirror-like surface reflects Aoraki/Mount Cook, New Zealand's tallest peak at 12,218 feet (3,724 meters). Helicopter tours, hikes atop the glacier, kayaking trips, scenic cruises, and even skydiving expeditions are just a few of the ways visitors soak in the mountain highs.

The entire region, known in the Maori language as Te Wahipounamu, extends as far south as Milford Sound, and has been a UNESCO World Heritage Site since 1990. In addition to its outstanding natural beauty, Te Wahipounamu's unique flora and fauna are evidence of how New Zealand broke away from the super-continent Gondwanaland before the evolution of marsupials and other mammals. Carnivorous land snails, flightless kiwis, and the kea, the world's only alpine parrot, are just a few of the species found nowhere else on Earth.

Between 1983 and 2008, Fox, Franz Josef, and some 50 other glaciers were actually advancing by several feet per year. Since then, however, both have resumed a century-long pattern of retreating, often

at rates as vertiginous as the glaciers themselves. The pullback has wiped out the gains made during the previous two decades, and scientists predict their complete disappearance by the end of this century.

Plan Your Trip

Location: South Island, New Zealand

Getting There: The two glaciers are about 30 minutes apart on the west coast of South Island. Whether you drive from Christchurch or Queenstown, allow five hours for the journey, because you'll want to stop frequently to admire the views.

When to Go: The weather at the glaciers is unpredictable year-round. It's generally warmer in summer (December–February), but that's also the high season, so expect crowds. The temperature rarely gets below freezing even in winter (June–August), and is usually more stable, resulting in crevasses and ice caves that don't melt in the midday sun. There are also a lot fewer visitors this time of year. The lower altitude of the towns means that they rarely get snow, even when the glaciers do, so driving is typically not treacherous.

Waitomo Glowworm Caves

Enjoy a natural light show in a subterranean grotto.

The dense concentrations of *arachnocampa luminosa*, a species unique to New Zealand, are the stars of the show here, lighting up the Waitomo caves with a blue bioluminescence unlike anything else you've ever seen. First discovered in 1871, the creatures were originally thought to be glowworms; after scientists realized they were actually fungus gnats, the cave's misnomer stuck.

The local Maori people have been providing tours of the Waitomo Caves for more than a century, making the caverns one of New Zealand's top tourist attractions. More than half a million people annually stroll down the circular staircase into the dark caves, marveling at the Cathedral chamber before boarding boats that carry them silently (glowworms hate noise) along the underground stream through the grotto.

There are all kinds of add-on adventures for adrenaline junkies, including ziplining, abseiling (a.k.a. rappelling), and blackwater rafting through underground rapids below a sky of glowworms.

The greatest threat to this natural light show is people, and not just the ones who touch the limestone formations with oily fingers or break off a stalactite to take home as a souvenir. The mere presence of humans brings carbon dioxide to the caves, which can reduce the humidity levels required for the glowworms to survive and corrode the limestone.

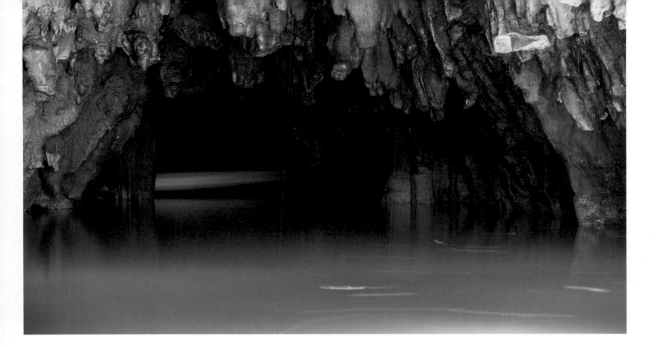

There are carbon dioxide monitors in the caves, so you won't have to hold your breath for the length of your visit. But you might leave disappointed if you arrive on a day when the caves are completely shut because CO_2 levels are too high (something that happens just a handful of times every year). You *can* do your part to ensure the glowworms are here for another 150 years, however, by not bringing light into the caves, walking only on designated walkways, and holding on to handrails rather than cave walls.

Plan Your Trip

Location: North Island, New Zealand

Getting There: Waitomo Caves are about a 2.5-hour drive south of Auckland, the country's largest city.

When to Go: The temperature inside the caves is a steady 61°F (16°C) year-round, so any time of year is a good time to visit. You'll experience smaller crowds (and less chance of a CO_2 shutdown) if you visit on a weekday.

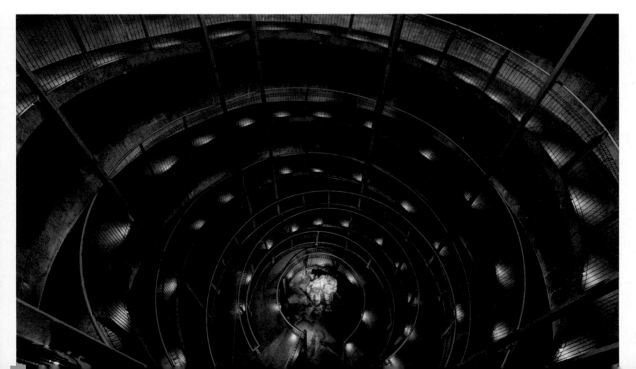

French Polynesia

Escape to the quintessential tropical island paradise.

Tahiti, Bora Bora, Moorea—just mentioning these places conjures up images of the quintessential tropical island escape. These islands are the stars of French Polynesia and the stuff of vacation fantasies.

Bungalows floating on stilts hover above clear turquoise waters teeming with tropical fish, visible through a glass-bottomed floor. Room service breakfast can be delivered via outrigger canoe. Soft

sand beaches fringe tranquil blue lagoons beneath a skyline of spiky volcanic mountains.

Throughout the islands, you're never far from a hammock, lounge chair, or bed on which to while the day away. More taxing pursuits include snorkeling and diving the endless coral reefs, boating from one island to another, riding a jeep to hidden waterfalls ending in placid swimming holes, or hiking through pineapple fields and verdant valleys to unparalleled vistas. And the food is everything you expect when French chefs get to work with fresh seafood and tropical produce.

The land and its people inspired the colorful works of the French painter Paul Gauguin, who spent most of the last decade of his life here. His grave and a reproduction of the house he last lived in are located on the even more remote island of Hiva Oa, nearly 900 miles from Tahiti. It's a reminder that French Polynesia is so much more than its most-visited destinations. Half of its 118 islands are uninhabited, giving visitors abundant opportunities to lose themselves in paradise.

If sea level rises even half as much as scientists currently predict over the next few decades,

however, many of those overwater bungalows may become underwater ones. Flooding is already commonplace. The threat is serious enough that French Polynesia in 2017 agreed to locate floating artificial islands powered by wind and solar energy off their coasts.

Plan Your Trip

Location: South Pacific Ocean

Getting There: Tahiti is the largest island in French Polynesia and the location of its major international airport, near the capital of Papeete. From there, you can take a ferry to Moorea, or a connecting flight to Bora Bora, Huahine, Rangiroa, and other more remote islands.

When to Go: It's always warm in French Polynesia, but it rains more often between November and April. July and August have the best weather, but the most crowds, as Tahitians often take time off in those months to vacation on outer islands. May, June, September, and October are a sweet spot where good weather, smaller crowds, and lower prices on airfares and hotels converge.

Kiribati

Get on island time.

Kiribati is an independent nation of 33 islands scattered across an area the size of India in the central Pacific Ocean. History buffs might recall that its capital, Tarawa, was the site of one of the bloodiest battles of World War II.

Visitors to today's Kiribati (pronounced Kiribas) encounter no warring U.S. and Japanese soldiers, although relics and fortresses from the historic battle remain on several islands. Instead, they'll find a remote and largely undeveloped group of atolls, home to friendly people and eye-opening adventures for the right traveler.

Big game fishing expeditions for marlin, sailfish, and giant trevally are a main attraction for visitors to Kiribati; most trips leave from Tarawa.

Kiritimati Island, some 2,000 miles (3,288 km) to the east, is one of the few places in the world where you can fight bonefish in saltwater. Kiritimati is also a beacon for migrating seabirds, including the endemic Christmas Island Warbler and the endangered Phoenix Petrel.

On nearby Fanning (a.k.a. Tabuaeran) Island, surfers have consistently impressive swells all to themselves nearly year-round. And the snorkeling and scuba diving throughout Kiribati are as astonishing as you'd expect from remote coral atolls in the Pacific.

Unfortunately, most of Kiribati's islands sit no more than 10 feet (3 meters) above sea level. Already two of those islands—Abanuea and Tebua

Tarawa, both uninhabited, thankfully—were swallowed by the Pacific Ocean at the end of the 1990s. If, as scientists predict, the oceans rise by just 2.6 feet (0.8 meters), nearly the entire country will be underwater by the year 2100. The Kiribati government has allowed 75 people per year to migrate to New Zealand and has purchased land in nearby Fiji should all 120,000 of Kiribati's residents have to evacuate.

Plan Your Trip

Location: Central Pacific Ocean

Getting There: Tarawa Airport is a three-hour flight from Fiji or five hours from Brisbane, Australia. Kiritimati Island is a three-hour flight from Honolulu or a five-hour flight from Fiji. Flights are not available every day.

When to Go: Kiribati has a hot tropical climate, with both air and water temperatures rarely varying much from a pleasant 85°F (29°C) year-round. Rain falls year-round, but more so in the rainy season from December to April, when cyclones can be a concern. September, October, and November are the driest months.

Federated States of Micronesia

Explore the ruins of 800-year-old cities and 80-year-old wars.

This independent nation of more than 600 islands (spanning more than 1,500 miles/2,414 km in the Pacific Ocean) is one of the most remote places on the planet. Getting there from any continent is a day-long journey. But that distance is part of Micronesia's appeal: nobody comes here by accident, so there's never a crowded beach. English is widely spoken, and the U.S. dollar is the local currency.

Almost all of Micronesia's population lives on four islands: Pohnpei, Chuuk, Yap, and Kosrae. Pohnpei is home to Micronesia's capital city (Palikir), its biggest city (Kolonia), and its oldest city, 800-year-old Nan Madol, a settlement often referred to as the Venice of the Pacific for the dozens of canals connecting its man-made islets. Comparisons to Stonehenge and Peru's Sacsayhuaman might be equally apt, as nobody is quite sure how the giant

boulders (some weighing more than 50 tons) were put in place. Nan Madol has been a UNESCO World Heritage site since 2016.

Chuuk (formerly known as Truk) is best known for ruins of a more recent vintage: divers can explore more than 70 Japanese World War II shipwrecks, plane-wrecks, and submarine-wrecks off Chuuk's shores. Yap is renowned for its large coin-like stones and waterways through mangrove forests that are great for exploring by kayak. Hikers, meanwhile, might opt for Kosrae, where they can trek the challenging trail to the cloud forest atop Mt. Finkol (elevation 2,064 feet/629 meters).

Rising sea levels are not some future threat to Micronesia's inhabitants; they're a clear and present danger. The ocean has already claimed several uninhabited coral atolls in the archipelago

and is nipping at the shores of larger islands that *are* populated. Scientists believe the situation will become even more acute, because the ocean here is rising three times as fast as the worldwide average of 3 mm (0.1 inches) per year.

Plan Your Trip

Location: South Pacific Ocean

Getting There: Each of Micronesia's four major islands has an international airport. Pohnpei International is the largest, welcoming the most flights from other countries.

When to Go: The temperature throughout Micronesia remains around 82°F (28°C) year-round. December through February is the dry season. You might plan your trip to coincide with Yap Day (March 1), an annual celebration of all things Yapese. July is a busy time of year, even though it falls during the rainy season.

Palawan

Is this the best island in the entire world? You decide.

Choosing a favorite island in the Philippines could take an entire lifetime. After all, there are more than 7,000 of them. But you'd be forgiven if you never got past Palawan, a cigar-shaped island at the western edge of the Philippine archipelago, surrounded by 1,800 islets, keys, atolls, and other tropical nests. *Travel & Leisure*'s readers ranked it the best island in the entire world in 2013, 2017, and 2020.

What's not to love: crystal-clear, warm aquamarine waters give way to stunning white sand beaches backed by limestone cliffs and other intricate rock formations. Countless bays and lagoons shelter semi-secret beaches and grottoes. Laid-back fishing villages prevail throughout the islands, populated by locals who are routinely assessed as some of the happiest and friendliest people on the planet.

Palawan is also home to two UNESCO World Heritage sites and three other natural treasures protected within the Palawan UNESCO Biosphere Reserve. The most renowned is the Puerto Princesa Subterranean River, a 15-mile (24-km) sea cave

through limestone karst. In 2012, it was named one of the New7Wonders of Nature, a list based on 100 million internet votes.

Plan Your Trip

Location: Western Philippines, Pacific Ocean

Getting There: Ninoy Aquino International in Manila is the country's largest airport, where you can connect to a regional flight to Puerto Princesa or Busuanga/Coron. Several airlines also offer international flights to Cebu, which has regional connections to Palawan.

When to Go: January is the ideal month to visit. The weather is cooler and less humid, the holiday crowds have largely gone home, and there are relatively few rainy days. January is also when some of the country's best festivals take place, including Sinulog, a religious celebration in Cebu accompanied by secular street parties and a grand parade; and Ati-Atihan, marked by colorful costumes, face painting, and dancing in the streets.

Palawan's other UNESCO site, Tubbataha Reefs National Park, is protected not only for its stellar marine life—more than half the world's coral species are found here—but also as a sanctuary for 100 bird species. The park is located 93 miles (150 km) off the coast in the Sulu Sea, but you don't have to travel that far for exceptional snorkeling and diving. Countless Palawan beaches afford opportunities to see similarly brilliant displays of tropical fish.

Climate change is a serious threat to Palawan (not to mention most of the Philippines, whose 10 largest municipalities are all coastal). Higher global temperatures mean more heat waves in summer, sea level rise, stronger typhoons and tropical cyclones, and more frequent flooding and drought. In December 2021, Typhoon Rai (known locally as Typhoon Odette) turned most of the trees at Puerto Princesa National Park from green to brown and caused more than $1 billion worth of damage to roads, streets, businesses, and homes. Slash-and-burn farming, timber-poaching, and mining are also a threat to the forests of Mt. Mantalingahan in southern Palawan.

Antarctica

Journey to the bottom of the world.

The seventh continent truly is Earth's final frontier, a forbiddingly remote destination, owned by no one and populated only by temporary-resident researchers and support staff. The lack of civilization at the icy landmass surrounding the world's southern pole makes for a hauntingly quiet, undeveloped place to hike, kayak, or simply admire from the deck of a cruise ship.

This stunning landscape of icy seas, snow-covered mountains, and breathtaking glaciers is also habitat for a surprisingly diverse collection of wildlife. Humpback whales, orcas, and a half dozen other species can be found in Antarctica's waters, often coming close enough to rock your dinghy. Seals bask on the sea ice, secure in the knowledge that they have no predators on land. And then, of course, there are the penguins, eight different kinds of them, ranging from the 20-inch rockhoppers to the four-foot-tall emperors, the stars of the hit 2005 documentary *March of the Penguins*.

Plan Your Trip

Location: Antarctica

Getting There: Most Antarctic cruises depart from Ushuaia in southern Argentina, which is a three-hour flight from Buenos Aires. You can also get to Ushuaia by land (and a ferry across the Magellan Strait) from Punta Arenas, Chile. It is also possible to fly from Punta Arenas to Antarctica's King George Island. This is an expensive option, but it avoids a sea crossing of the Drake Passage, which can be a nauseating voyage for those prone to seasickness in some weather conditions.

When to Go: Ships can only navigate Antarctica's waters between November and March. That's summer in the southern hemisphere, but temperatures still rarely rise above freezing. November is mating season for both penguins and seals. December brings days with 20 hours of sunlight and calving glaciers, but also holiday crowds. Penguin chicks start to hatch in January; February is best for whale watching.

Except for the blue whale, none of Antarctica's species is listed as endangered or even threatened. But rising ocean temperatures are melting its glaciers and sea ice at an alarming rate, which, in turn, causes sea levels to rise even more. According to one 2021 study, the changes are even affecting the shape of Earth's crust. And as global fisheries become depleted, pressure will mount to open the Antarctic to fishing.

About the Author

John Rosenthal is the author of *The World Almanac Road-Tripper's Guide to National Parks*, the *AAA Guide to Boston and New England*, and *Hawaii for Dummies* (6th edition). In his 35 years as a travel journalist, he has written about small-ship cruises of Alaska for *The New York Times*, sheep-herding trials in Ireland for *The Washington Post*, and driving through the American Southwest for *National Geographic Traveler*, where he was a contributing editor. He lives in Los Angeles, where he regularly hikes with his wife and his Labrador Retriever, Marcy.